Stand Strong

in college

Alex McFarland

A Focus on the Family book published by
Tyndale House Publishers, Inc., Carol Stream, Illinois 60188

Focus on the Family and the accompanying logo and design are federally registered
trademarks of Focus on the Family, Colorado Springs, CO 80995.

TYNDALE and Tyndale's quill logo are registered trademarks of Tyndale House
Publishers, Inc.

All Scripture quotations, unless otherwise indicated, are taken from the *Holy Bible, New
International Version*®. NIV®. Copyright © 1973, 1978, 1984 by International Bible
Society. Used by permission of Zondervan Publishing House. All rights reserved. Scripture quotations marked (KJV) are taken from the *King James Version*. Scripture quotations marked (NKJV) are taken from the *New King James Version*. Copyright © 1982
by Thomas Nelson, Inc. Used by permission. All rights reserved.

People's names and certain details of their stories have been changed to protect the pri-
vacy of the individuals involved.

Editor: Marianne Hering
Cover design by Joseph Sapulich
Cover photograph of people © by Eric Skorupa/iStockphoto. All rights reserved.
Cover image treatments © iStockphoto. All rights reserved.

Library of Congress Cataloging-in-Publication Data
McFarland, Alex, 1964-
  Stand strong : in college / by Alex McFarland.
     p. cm.
  "Focus on the Family."
  Includes bibliographical references.
  ISBN-13: 978-1-58997-465-4
  ISBN-10: 1-58997-465-4
  1. College students—Religious life. I. Title.
  BV4531.3.M4195 2007
  248.8'34—dc22

                                    2007017275

Printed in the United States of America
1 2 3 4 5 6 7 8 9 / 13 12 11 10 09 08 07

*This book is dedicated to peanut butter,
and to my favorite brand, Harris Teeter,
which has nutritiously seen many a student
through college and through life,
myself included.*

■   ■   ■

Be **STRONG** and take heart,
all you who hope in the LORD.
—*Psalm 31:24*

Contents

Acknowledgments

Books are not just written, they are built. This project has been dear to my heart for years, and many dedicated people deserve credit for helping me to hammer away at it. *Stand Strong in college* is based on a seminar I have presented in hundreds of churches around the United States, which was originally entitled "*What You'll Hear Your Freshman Year: Preparing for the Ways College Will Challenge Your Faith.*" I am indebted to a number of people who collaborated to help make this book a reality.

To the wonderful team that is Focus on the Family, I am grateful for Phil Hildebrand, Larry Weeden, Clark Miller, and Glenn Williams. Together, they gave me a precious gift: *opportunity*. Very special thanks go to the greatest editors any writer could have—Marianne Hering and Tom Neven. They are godly, gifted professionals who have taught me much. Other people at Focus on the Family who deserve special mention include Bruce Peppin, Kellie Vaughan, Chris Perez, and everyone at Global Resources, Briargate Media, and the M-group. I thank God for the blessings that come from working with Cheryl Wilhelmi, Bob Smithouser, Christina Loznicka, Lori Vande Griend, Bob Waliszewski, Clay Miller, Whitney Gilman, Laura Neff, and so many more.

Special appreciation goes to Joseph Sapulich at Tyndale for the outstanding cover design.

Gratitude is extended to EPA Award–winning journalist Warren Smith. He helped me write this book, and his contributions cannot be overstated. Also helping were the staff and faculty of Southern Evangelical Seminary and the Veritas Graduate School of Apologetics (http://www.ses.edu). Founder Norman Geisler, Academic Dean Barry Leventhal, Christina Woodside, Ron Jordal, Jason Reed, Cheryl Maddox, Kathy Njoya, Robert Kornegay, Lanny Wilson, Michelle Hitzelberger, Scott Matcherz, Brandon Dahm, Marcia Montenegro, Bill Roach, Chris Tweedt, and Ted Wright all deserve special mention.

Several key friends in ministry deserve special acknowledgment. These include: Broadcaster and author Danny Fontana, and engineers Casey Shannon and Bo Thompson. Thanks, guys, for graciously allowing me to use your *iLife* studios each Friday afternoon and for staying after hours just so I could broadcast *Truth Talk Live*. Special thanks also go out to Stu Epperson, Jr., my friend of many years and founder of *Truth Broadcasting*.

I am also very grateful for Ron Shuping, Doug Butts, Karen Mathis, and the staff of the Inspiration Television Network. Thank you for having the vision to reach teens with the biblical worldview, and thank you for giving me a platform as host of *Take a Stand*.

Two awesome brothers who have shaped my life in a number of ways are Lee Strobel and Mark Mittelberg. I thank the Lord for you both.

I praise God for my wife, Angie, who has prayed for me, helped me, and driven me to and from the airport at crazy hours of the day. In addition to being a nurse, she often helped to look after my parents while I was away speaking. Thank you, Angie.

I am thankful to Jesus Christ for saving me, and for the Bible, which for 22 years has been an ever-present friend.

Finally, I acknowledge and applaud the Christians present on college campuses everywhere: the professors, staff, and students who choose to stand strong.

Call It as God Sees It

It's weird. By the end of my senior year in high school, I just felt like I had so outgrown my church's student ministry, and I was practically dying to move on. College threw me a lot of challenges that I wasn't really expecting, and I had been probably one of the strongest Christians in my whole youth group. Now I think about how I could have been a lot more focused on the Lord while I had the time, and while I was pretty much surrounded by adults who cared about my spiritual growth. I feel like most everybody on campus would just as soon we Christians all become atheists.

—*Kyle T., Texas*

In the Broadway smash hit *Guys and Dolls*, gamblers Nathan Detroit and Sky Masterson made their living by holding illegal gambling games. Over the years, they won and lost thousands upon thousands of dollars rolling dice. During one gambling session, a fellow hoodlum objected to Nathan's specially made dice: "May I have a look at them? These dice ain't got no spots on 'em! They're blank!"

Nathan reassures the fellow con he need not worry: "I had the spots removed," he says. "But I remember where the spots formerly were."

It's no surprise the blank dice always end up rolling in Nathan's favor.[1]

This illustration has parallels to real life—a more serious "game" with higher stakes than anything money can buy. Today many people have decided life is a game of "Call It as You See It." The goal is to fight your way ahead, make up the rules as you go, and change them when needed.

Judges 21:25 confirms that even in ancient times, people were prone to doing what was right in their own eyes. That philosophy is as spiritually empty now as it was then. During your college years and on, you will have to decide if you are going to live by the world's rules, which are really no rules at all, or if you are going to live according to God's truth. Are you going to pursue conformity or character? Convictions or convenience?

Good-bye High School, Hello World

This book is for those who want to learn to call life as God sees it.

This book is for you if you are in college and you now know that if you are going to get the most out of your college experience you have only a few years left to take control. Perhaps you are a high school junior or senior, or you've just graduated from high school, and you're looking at college with both excitement and anxiety. This book can help set you on the right course.

Stand Strong in college is not your normal get-ready-for-college book. It's not designed to help you with your applications, references, SATs, ACTs, or your application essay—at least not directly. Rather, the purpose of this book is to convince you that you can and should determine today what your college experience will look like tomorrow. The choices you make now and in the near future will have an impact on the rest of your life.

One of my professors in grad school, Dr. E. L. Towns, used to say, "You are purchasing your tomorrows today." The passage of time is so subtle that most of us barely notice this truth. Morphing from youth-grouper to successful college student to adult disciple is a challenge, yet believers must be good stewards of both their present and future. I hope and pray this book will help you realize that the time to invest in all that God intends you to be is *now.*

A term that has become popular in recent years when speaking about successful transitioning through college, moving into a career, and reaching maturity as a young adult is "preparing to launch." That term is all wrapped up in finances, independence, and worldly achievement. But personal goals and the desire for success must never blind us from the reality that we belong to God. The most important step in truly preparing to launch is to reaffirm your total commitment to Jesus Christ. He controls our destiny because, of course, Jesus is sovereign over our parents and circumstances, too. Psalm 31:15 promises that our "times" are in God's hands. Don't bet your life on anything or anyone less trustworthy than the Creator who formed you for His glory and purposes. The goal of this book is to teach you how to live your life by God's rules, to call it as God sees it.

Part I

A Prepared Heart

My God is my rock, in whom I take refuge,
my shield and the horn of my salvation. He is
my **strong**hold, my refuge and my savior—from
violent men you save me.

—*2 Samuel 22:3*

When I began college, I played by my rules.

I chose my school because it was close to home.

I chose my major because I wanted to be a writer (and avoid math).

I chose my friends to have fun.

My heart was mine, and I devoted it to living for the moment, doing everything humanly possible to pack that moment with fun.

At the time, the most important thing to me was music. I just knew one day I would get a big break and get discovered; until then I played guitar in any small-time oldies band that would take me. Before, during, and after our performances, I would drink and drink a lot. Most times I'd end up drunk.

One Friday night in late October, I drank heavily after a gig at a frat party. I passed out, and some of the frat guys threw me in a Dumpster behind an Italian restaurant. Around nine the next morning, I woke to the smell of soured spaghetti. It took a few seconds before I realized where I was. In a few more I realized a Dumpster was where I belonged. I felt like trash. I was treating myself like trash. Why not throw my life away?

About nine months later, I gave my life to Christ. I came back to college with a whole different outlook, purpose, and goal. My Savior had changed my heart forever.

As I began to grow in my faith, one of the strongest feelings in my heart was gratitude to Christ for having kept me alive during the wild, meaningless years. I thought about two of my friends who had died in alcohol-related accidents and knew it could easily have happened to me. Uncertainty about their spiritual condition haunted me. I was extremely grateful to Jesus Christ for being so patient with me as He brought me to Himself. The Lord had changed my heart and began to reorder my priorities. I wanted my life to become a decades-long thank-you note back to Him.

I pray none of you ever wakes up in a garbage Dumpster. But hear this: Anything you do that is not done for Christ has no eternal value—it's garbage whether it comes in the form of a six-figure income, a guy with six-pack abs, or the honor of graduating *magna cum laude*.

I see many teens who claim to be Christians but whose hearts are still in the world. They try to have it both ways; they want acceptance by their secular peers and with Jesus. They tell me they're unfulfilled. They might try changing majors, but what they really need is to let Jesus change their hearts.

Christians, all of our victories or defeats are essentially spiritual in nature. Therefore, the most important college and life preparation of all relates to our eternal relationship with Christ.

That is the heart of the matter, and that is where we begin.

Chapter 1

Do You Have What It Takes?

The LORD is the **strong**hold of my life.

—*Psalm 27:1*

I know the Bible says pride is a sin. But I'll confess I was a proud youth pastor when, in 1995, I watched as some of my most dedicated leaders graduated from high school.

They were six of the most outstanding young men and women in our church. And I had poured myself into them during the preceding few years. All six were going off to college. All six had a vital faith in Christ. All six had everything I knew to teach them at that time.

But today these six are adults, and only two of the six are still actively, enthusiastically following the Lord.

What Went Wrong?

Researchers knew what I didn't at the time—even good youth group kids fall away from the church once they reach college age. Consider these statistics:

- Only one out of three evangelical teens say, "The church will play a significant role in my life once I leave home."[1]

- Between 70 and 94 percent of evangelical teens are leaving the traditional church after high school, and very few ever return.[2]
- Ninety-eight percent of professed born-again youth and adults say, "I believe in Jesus Christ," but their actions, attitudes, lifestyle, behavioral patterns, and life goals do not reflect New Testament, biblical Christlikeness.[3]
- Only one-fifth of twentysomethings have maintained a level of spiritual activity consistent with their high school experiences.[4]

A peek behind the statistics

The news was not all bad with my youth group's first graduating class. In fact, sometimes I tell myself that if I were a major league ball player, I'd probably be an all-star. Two out of six is a .333 batting average! That's pretty good.

But these are not base hits. These are human lives.

What I've learned from my own experience, interviews with college students, and from listening to other youth pastors is this: What happens to students *in the first six months* after they graduate from high school has huge consequences in their lives. The ramifications can affect even the lives of their children.

Yes, during that graduation week of 1995, I was impressed by the spiritual commitment of the students in our group. I was happy about things I saw the Lord doing in their lives. But now I know I should have been a bit less proud and a bit more aggressive in making sure they were ready for the challenging college years that lay ahead.

What went wrong with my kids and what is going wrong in our colleges today? I've asked myself that question a thousand times, and I've asked hundreds of youth pastors and thousands of teens that same question. The answers are as varied as there are people, but there are patterns. No one suddenly wakes up in the morning and announces,

"Today is the day I flush my faith." Emotional traps can lead teens away from the church more quickly than you'd think. Look around you at the next youth group meeting. Imagine that 80 percent of the seniors in the room will stop going to church within the next four years. Who will go, and who will stay? It's difficult to predict.

For years I have had the privilege of crisscrossing the country, speaking to teens throughout the nation. In getting to know countless students, I have come to recognize some predictable patterns. I'd like to summarize a few details from the lives of some teens I've known along the journey.

Let me introduce you to six EVERYTEENS who will represent good youth group kids. Throughout the book, we'll watch them during their freshman year in college to see how they fare spiritually, academically, socially, and emotionally. We'll look at what affects them and how those challenges will change the course of their lives.

EVERYTEEN Adam is a natural leader, Becuse he is handsome and athletic, youth pastors love to have Adam in a youth group. Other kids will come just to hang out with him. Not quite talented enough for an athletic scholarship, and not quite brilliant enough for an academic scholarship, he is nonetheless sought after by colleges who love his well-rounded capabilities. Adam has a full scholarship to a Christian university.

EVERYTEEN Cameron is the most intellectually gifted of the group. He is the valedictorian of one of the largest high schools in his state. He is off to a major university in Indiana and wants to study law. Voted "most likely to go into politics" by his senior class, Cameron can articulate the tenets of the faith almost as well as his pastor.

EVERYTEEN David is your average kid. He does well in math and science classes, but also enjoys reading literature. He was a regular at youth group, helping with the worship band setup and takedown. He's going to a state college, where he will study accounting.

EVERYTEEN Erin is a new Christian. She began coming to youth group at Christmastime when a girl from the swim team invited her. She is going to a division one school on a partial water polo scholarship. Her parents are hoping she'll outgrow her newfound friends and crazy ideas at college.

EVERYTEEN Joel recently found out the roommate assigned to him is a Mormon. That's okay with him, because the roommate describes himself as quiet and studious. Perfect. Joel didn't party in high school and is entering a small liberal arts college with the goal of avoiding that whole scene. He has already contacted the InterVarsity Christian Fellowship and has the phone numbers of two student leaders.

EVERYTEEN Megan, like Adam, has great leadership potential. She is the salutatorian of her large senior class and has been accepted at several colleges, including a couple of schools rated among the top 300 in the country. At high school, she has many friends. She is that smart girl, the outspoken Christian, the student-council leader who somehow manages to avoid the "geek" label.

What's in Your Spiritual Bank Account?

You wouldn't be reading this book if you weren't serious about your spiritual growth and want to make the most of your college experience. You can probably tell that I am passionate about teens going deep with the Lord and becoming everything that God intends.

You may be more ready for college than you realize. A lot of people have been investing in you since you were born—you didn't get where you are today all by yourself. Additionally, God has given you spiritual resources and He expects you to use them. Let's call both of those things "spiritual capital." Let's compare such spiritual capital to the accumulation of wealth and becoming financially secure. A popular television commercial for a credit card asks the question,

"What's in your wallet?" The advertiser suggests that with its card, you'll have the buying power you need to meet the expenses of life, and you'll have protection against high interest rates.

I'm certainly not advocating that brand of credit card or, for that matter, credit cards of any kind. But I do like the question: "What's in your wallet?" As you prepare to go off to college, what do you have tucked away, so to speak, to see you through the challenges that life will have for you in the years ahead?

I believed I had sent my students off to college with what they needed. I've discovered you'll need resources in four important areas if you are to withstand the challenges you will encounter in college and beyond. Those four are academic, social, emotional, and spiritual. These areas are so important that I will devote an entire chapter to each. For right now, a quick overview will do.

Academic Challenges. Most people who lose their faith during college usually don't reject Christianity because they were unprepared for academic rigor. So while the academic indicators are important

Overheard in the Student Lounge

Don't think that you can necessarily lean on the thing that made you strong in high school. Unless it was the Lord, of course. I mean, in high school some people were good at sports, or they were superpopular, or their parents were always helping them out. That's okay, but remember those things won't be there. Or at least not as easily accessible. You have to become self-reliant and God-reliant.

—*Anonymous, Liberty University, Virginia*

Alex on His Soapbox

Dorothy was right. "There's no place like home." A recent study took a scientific look at the homesickness experienced by teens once they move out.

"Leaving home is a universal developmental milestone," said the January 2007 issue of *Pediatrics*, the journal of the American Academy of Pediatrics. This study documented that 95 percent of young people become homesick once they leave for college. A few (about 1 in 14) will suffer acute, debilitating homesickness that seriously impairs their ability to function.

Larkin was the only girl in a family with three brothers. "In our house growing up, having your own 'space' or time alone was pretty rare," she says. By her senior year, Larkin was excited at the prospect of leaving for a college campus hundreds of miles away. But settling in to her freshman year, Larkin was surprised at the intensity of her homesickness. "I made friends fairly easily, and I got to know a lot of people on a superficial level," she says. "More than once I cried and prayed myself to sleep because of loneliness. Being away from my family and surroundings was not as great as I thought it would be."

There is nothing wrong with admitting you're homesick and lonely; such emotions are part of being human. Recognizing the near universality of homesickness (95 percent) is all the more reason to be intentional about reaching out to others, making friends on campus, finding fellow Christians, and getting plugged in to a church. Seek someone who needs encouragement—you'll end up being encouraged, too.[5]

and shouldn't be neglected, other reasons should compel you to do well in college, such as gaining character and wisdom. When you study hard, you are not only learning the subject, you are learning discipline. If you develop those skills early, you will find yourself well prepared to face the intellectual challenges of life after college.

Social Challenges. There's something about being a senior in high school. Even if you go to a big high school or you're not particularly popular or well-known, just being a senior confers a certain status. You're a big fish in a small pond. But college is different. You're back to being a freshman. It's likely that the college you attend will be many times larger than your high school. You may see some of your classmates only once a week. How do you develop friendships in this environment? While you are away from family and longtime friends, who will really be there when you're lonely or just need to talk? Where will you find trustworthy people?

Emotional Challenges. When things go well, it's not hard to deal with life, to remain upbeat and positive. But what happens when social and academic challenges of college get the better of you? And, trust me, they get the better of us all from time to time.

Part of emotional health is being able to maintain an emotional even keel during the storms of life and avoid making decisions that are motivated by fear or desperation. In the King James Version of the Bible, Colossians 2:10 says that the believer is "complete" in Christ. That's how we are in Christ—full and complete. We may not always *feel* that way, and circumstances can certainly conspire to make us feel like a loser. But don't cave in to those emotions, because if you forget about your blessed standing in Christ, it may lead to less-than-ideal decision-making.

Spiritual Challenges. As important and challenging as these other three areas are, they rate a distant second, third, and fourth to the challenges you will face in your spiritual life. It sounds a bit odd to say it this way, but the worst academic or social decision you make might affect your life for years, or decades, or even your whole life. But when you die, that will be the end of it. The spiritual choices you make will affect you for all eternity.

A secular college can be a dangerous place for the unprepared because it is full of people who pride themselves in offering spiritual challenges to other people. It is a place where destroying someone's Christian faith is considered a virtue.

Count on this: Your faith will be challenged. Your mission—our mission together during the course of this book—will be to give you the tools to help you fight that challenge and emerge victorious.

Preparing Your Heart

I told you that two of my six were still following the Lord, and that's so. My point is not that some people are bailing on their commitment to the Lord. That happens in every generation. The real news is you don't have to be one of them. A consistent Christian walk through college and into adulthood can happen for you. God promised to never leave nor forsake us (Hebrews 13:5). Jesus overcame the tribulations of this world (John 16:33), and He promised that nothing could separate believers from His protective care (John 10:28). Let's look at what God will give you to prepare your heart for the college experience.

Your family
God can use whatever type of family you have as a foundation for a successful college life. If your family is able to support you financially,

emotionally, or spiritually then rejoice and use those resources wisely and thank God for them. If your family doesn't offer you that kind of support, don't despair. You can learn early to trust God for your needs, and your faith will be built up. He is able to supply all of your needs beyond what you can ask or even imagine (Philippians 4:19; Ephesians 3:20).

Your educational background

As you prepare for college, you may have some insecurity about whether you can hack it at this next, much more advanced level. That's understandable. But let me remind you that for all kinds of reasons, from financial to a concern for their reputations, colleges are not to the business of seeing their students fail. If you have been accepted to a college, someone there—and probably many someones—believes that you can succeed and be a positive representative of that institution for

---

A Word from the Faculty

Maintain close relationships with your parents, treating them as advisors whose counsel you respect (even if they aren't Christians). Be committed to church involvement before you go to college and once you get there. Don't switch from church to church. Don't miss a Sunday if you can at all help it. Volunteer to minister in your church in some way, join a small group Bible study of some kind. These things will keep you committed and accountable.

—*Anonymous, professor of philosophy at a public university in the Midwest*

years to come. They believe you have what it takes—whether you believe it or not!

God's Word

The Bible is a rich source of wisdom and practical knowledge. It is also the Word of God. By daily listening to what God's Word is saying to us, the world slowly, inevitably starts to make more sense. Life's challenges, though new and seemingly overwhelming, are neither surprising nor overwhelming to God.

Other Christians

You are not alone. Just as God is at work in your life, He is also at work in the lives of others. Some college campuses can be difficult places for Christians—incredibly difficult places. Once I led my youth group in an outreach event near a college that had originally been founded by a Christian. The history of this particular century-old college was entrenched in church work, and the denomination that had birthed this school still had a presence on campus. Sounds great, right? Imagine our shock when we learned that there was a "clothing optional" dorm on this formerly religious campus!

We learned about this in talking with some concerned Christian students who were faithfully representing Christ on their campus. Yes, "clothing optional" turned out to mean exactly what we thought. Yes, comparisons to Sodom and Gomorrah did come up in conversation! No, none of our ministry team went in!

But even in such extreme environments, I have yet to run across even the most secular campus where there were not dedicated, godly Christians who are serious about their spiritual health and the spiritual health of others. Seek them out, and you can be sure they will be happy to have you in their fellowship.

The Holy Spirit

Every Christian believer has the Holy Spirit living in him or her. Think about that! The God who spoke the universe into existence, who overcame death, who performed all manner of miracles—that very God lives in you. Now, I want to be clear that the Holy Spirit is

By the Book

Blessed is the man
    who does not walk in the counsel of the wicked
or stand in the way of sinners
    or sit in the seat of mockers.
But his delight is in the law of the LORD,
    and on his law he meditates day and night.
He is like a tree planted by streams of water,
    which yields its fruit in season
and whose leaf does not wither.
    Whatever he does prospers.

—*Psalm 1:1-3*

▪ ▪ ▪

Education is not the filling of a pail, but the lighting of a fire.
—*William Butler Yeats, Irish Nobel–Prize–winning playwright and poet (1865–1939)*[6]

▪ ▪ ▪

If any of you lacks wisdom, he should ask God, who gives generously to all without finding fault, and it will be given to him.
—*James 1:5*

not some sort of cosmic errand boy who will do what you want Him to do. No, just the opposite. The Holy Spirit's role is to give you the power to do what God wants you to do. But the good news is that as you mature, your will and God's will become more and more aligned, and the power of the Holy Spirit will be even more real to you.

The example of Jesus

It's a huge comfort to me to look at the life of Jesus and know that He faced all of the challenges I have ever faced, or will ever face, and He emerged victorious. The question "What Would Jesus Do?" has been overused, but the reason is because it's a good one. When I face a difficult situation, I often ask myself that question. It often gives me the courage to make the right choice here and now.

The Most Significant Investment
of All . . . Your Life

Have you ever heard of a CD or a mutual fund? Advertisements for such financial products often include someone asking a broker, "What's my expected ROI?" The "ROI," your "return on investment," is obviously an important consideration. As you set goals, make plans, and daily purchase your tomorrows, remember that the greatest returns will come from investments you've made with God.

To carry the investment analogy even further, we may legitimately raise the issue of "risks." There will be physical, academic, emotional, and spiritual challenges during your college years and afterward. But if you take an honest spiritual inventory, you'll probably discover that you have tremendous resources at your disposal. In the pages ahead we'll examine them in more depth, because my goal is not merely for you to survive, but to thrive and be victorious during your college years.

So, back to the question of that credit card commercial: What's in your wallet? The answer is a lot, more than enough to meet the challenges before you. But before we strategize about wisely investing your spiritual capital, I want to make sure you understand a few key ideas—even if you forget everything else in this book.

So turn the page and I'll tell you what they are!

Chapter 2

You Are Not Your Own

O Sovereign LORD, my **strong** deliverer,

who shields my head in the day of battle.

—*Psalm 140:7*

Though I wish I had become a Christian when I was a child, in some ways becoming a Christian in college has given me an opportunity to understand what my life would have been like without Jesus. If you can picture a train wreck in your mind, that about sums it up. After I became a Christian, I went back to school with a new reason to live and a new value system because *I was not my own.* I had been bought with a price (1 Corinthians 6:19-20), and my life belonged totally to Jesus. As I mentioned before, I wanted everything I did in life to become a decades-long thank-you to Jesus.

The concept of giving your whole heart and life to Jesus is so multifaceted and magnificent that I can't begin to cover the entire scope of it, even if I could say I have arrived at a perfect surrender, which I can't. For the scope of this book, however, we'll have to begin somewhere. So I'm introducing three concepts, which, if you can understand and implement, will help you throughout your college years and beyond.

1. Life is about stewardship, not ownership. (God owns everything.)
2. Every possible argument against Christianity has an answer.
3. A biblical worldview will help you see God's powerful truth.

1. Stewardship: You Are Not Your Own

Going off to college is a true rite of passage. Let me tell you: Almost every aspect of your life will never be the same. Your relationship with your parents and other family members will change. Some of your best high school friends will drift away, and you'll make friends in college unlike any you've ever had. You probably already know that. In fact, if you have been paying attention at all, you not only know that, but you are both exhilarated and afraid of the prospects.

And if that is overwhelming, let me share with you the other side of the coin. Yes, you are taking on a great many responsibilities, and you will be allowed a great many more rights. But you may have had parents like mine, who often said to me as I was growing up, often in the presence of others: "No matter how big you get, you'll always be my little boy." When my parents said this to me, it embarrassed me,

Alex on His Soapbox

Remember what E. T. said: "Phone home." Good advice. And today it is easier than ever with cell phones and prepaid phone cards. It is so important to stay in close communication with your parents. Call every week. Years down the road you will look back and be thankful for the time spent. You need it, and your parents do, too.

but it was also a great comfort. It was a simple expression that told me who I was and, more important, where I belonged in the world.

You may not have been blessed with parents who embarrassed you in this way! But what you may not know is this: No matter how "grown up" you become, if you are a Christian, you will always be God's child.

Even if you are not a Christian you probably have a sense that there must be more to this life than just looking out for number one! On a purely biological level, the instinct to care for others is hardwired into us. At the core of their existence, animals have an instinct to care for their offspring and thereby perpetuate their species.

We humans have an even stronger sense. We want to make a difference, to leave our mark on the world. We make and build. I would argue that this impulse is God-given. God is the Creator of the universe, and we are made in His image. So we, too, are creators. The universe belongs to God, and we belong to Him, but in His great love for us He entrusted portions of His universe to us. In Scripture, we first see this in the book of Genesis, when God told Adam and Eve to tend the garden. Much later in Scripture, in 1 Corinthians 6:19, we are reminded: "You are not your own."

I say all of that to say this: You are not the owner, but the steward, of a life. God has given you gifts and abilities. He has given you a particular background. He has given you opportunities and a certain time on this earth. He has given you passions and desires. But He expects us to use all of these gifts wisely.

Enlarge your time horizon

To be a good steward, you must enlarge your time horizon. Scientists define the horizon as that place in your field of vision where the earth meets the sky. If you are standing in a field, the horizon might be a row of trees at the edge of the field. If you are on a hill in the Great

Plains, your horizon has enlarged significantly. If you stand on a 14,000-foot peak in the middle of the Rockies, it seems as if you can see forever! But notice one thing: Nothing about the earth or the sky has changed. What has changed is your position and perspective.

So it is with time horizons. When you were a baby, your time horizon was very short. You only cared about your next meal and only when you were hungry. As you got older, your time horizon expanded. You learned that certain behaviors had consequences—either positive or negative. You learned to work to make money to buy things you wanted. But as you prepare for college, your time horizons have to expand even more. You have to learn to think not just weeks or months into the future, but years and even decades.

That's why some of the tools or skills you may have used in the past to help you make decisions may not be as helpful to you as they once were. Let's take a set of fundamental questions: Should I go to college? Where should I go to college? What should I study? Here are a few of the *wrong* questions to ask when trying to make these decisions.

- Where are my friends applying?
- Where may I pledge an influential fraternity or sorority?
- Where did my parents attend?
- Which degree that will land me the most lucrative job?

One of the reasons these are the *wrong* questions should be obvious to you based on what we've already discussed. Because you belong to God, your primary concern should not be what your friends—or for that matter, anyone else—wants you to do. Your primary concern should be trying to discover what God has in store for you.

That's not to say that others, especially your parents, won't have helpful and wise things to say to you, but let me propose a few alternative questions to get you moving in the right direction.

- What decision will give me the greatest opportunities in life?
- What decision will give me the greatest job satisfaction?
- Where will I have the greatest influence for Christ?
- What will allow me the greatest opportunities for stewardship for God's kingdom?
- Where will I be able to most fully develop my gifts and talents?

Again, I'm not saying to ignore your parents and friends. In fact, I would say just the opposite. Parents and friends are important parts of the support structure God has put in your life, something I'll say much more about in the next chapter. But it's important that you're asking the right questions when you go to others for advice. God made *you* the steward of your time, your gifts, and your talents. Other people can and should be involved in the process, but part of taking on more adult privileges, the kind that will be available to you in college, is also taking on adult responsibilities.

In other words, when it comes to important decisions in your life, the buck stops with you!

Developing the whole person

Another vital aspect of responsible stewardship is an understanding that God is sovereign over all aspects of life. Our discussion of God's role as creator of the universe should have already suggested that idea to you. But the Bible makes it plain that everything belongs to God. Psalm 24:1 says, "The earth is the LORD's, and everything in it, the world, and all who live in it." This includes you and me. *God owns us.*

II. Every Argument Against Christianity Has an Answer

The second vital idea I want to make sure you understand before we get down to the nitty-gritty of preparing for college is this: Every possible argument against Christianity has an answer.

This is a vital idea for a number of reasons. First of all, one of the things you can be sure will happen to you in college, even at a Christian college, is that your faith will be challenged. You will be asked to defend aspects of your faith that you have either never thought about or just accepted as true. Questions like these:

- Did Jesus really exist?
- Is His resurrection really true or just a nice idea?
- Can the Bible be trusted? Is it really true?
- Aren't there contradictions in the Bible? Which parts should I believe?

And then there is the question that, in one form or another, is the follow-up to all of these questions: How do you know? How can you be sure?

And once confronted, you may have doubts yourself. You may ask yourself: "What if that's *not* true? Why *do* I believe that? How can I be sure?"

EVERYTEEN Joel

If you remember, Joel was attending a small liberal arts college. He was about to find out that having the Bible as the foundation of his faith was more important than he had previously thought.

Joel had been IM-ing his roommate, Marshal, throughout August, so upon meeting in September, they had a pretty good friendship established. The issue of religion came up quickly, too quickly for Joel. Marshal knew the Book of Mormon well and felt comfortable talking about his church's views.

Joel heard an earful about the different levels of heaven. Murderers and abortionists couldn't get in at all. But one key issue of confusion for Joel was that Marshal claimed "good" people could get into a certain level of heaven, even if they'd never confessed faith in Jesus. There were many more ideas that confused Joel. But the biggest hang-up for him was that Marshal was so nice, and his entire family, all eight of them, were committed to the Church of Jesus Christ of Latter-day Saints. Joel knew that if he had grown up in Marshal's family, he would be a devoted Mormon, too.

Does a person just grow up and accept his parents' religion, or do you have to choose? he wondered. *Can the Bible and the Book of Mormon both be true?*

Three roads ahead

All people must come to a juncture like this at some point in their lives. You may have already reached it. If you haven't, you certainly will early in your college career.

Faithlessness. For some people, the direction they turn is away from faith. They don't know the answers to these questions, and they don't know where to turn to get the answers. No one or nothing in their backgrounds provides them with a clue. And often there are people around them who have also turned away from faith, and, as the saying goes, misery loves company. These people are essentially recruited into faithlessness—they may even switch to another religion.

Following the road of faithlessness has always seemed foolish to me—and not because I'm a preacher. It's foolish for purely logical reasons. Think about it. We're talking about some of the most interesting and important questions that a person will ever encounter. We're talking about questions that have been thought about, argued about, discussed, and written about by the greatest minds in history. And then, just because you encounter a few tough questions that you don't know the answer to, you assume that all of Christianity must not be true. That just doesn't make sense. That would be like saying, "Because I don't understand how electricity works, I'm never going to replace burned-out lightbulbs."

Spiritual Pride. At the opposite end of the spectrum is spiritual pride. Spiritual pride says, "I know all the answers." I encounter this attitude too often in the church. Pastors, church leaders, even young people who have been to all the conferences and retreats. They have a "been there, done that, got the T-shirt" mentality that tends to shut them down from more learning.

But the Bible is clear about what happens to the proud. "Pride goes before destruction, a haughty spirit before a fall," the wise writer of Proverbs tells us (16:18). I can't tell you how many times I've seen good kids from solid, Bible-believing churches get in trouble with drugs, alcohol, sexual promiscuity, or just a general cooling of their faith—all because they assume that those kinds of things could never happen to them. They believed they were above all that.

I've now learned that *none* of us is "above all that." We can all stumble, at any time in our lives. That's why I begin each day in prayer and in the Word, and I look to surround myself with people who will hold me accountable to do the right thing—even when I would rather have people around me who would just let me do what I please!

Faithfulness. Where I hope you end up is neither faithless nor proud, but faithful. The person of mature faith takes the questions I posed above seriously, because they are serious and important questions. But rather than throw up his hands in despair or become satisfied with "easy believism," the faithful person digs deeply into these questions and finds answers.

Answering all the questions that you are likely to encounter is well beyond the scope of this book, but I do want to say this: I have made it my life's work to explore these questions deeply. I have a graduate degree in theology that I pursued because these questions were important to me, and I, too, wanted answers. I have spoken to literally tens of thousands of college students on campuses all across the country, and I can with confidence say that every single objection that I have heard raised against Christianity can be met with a satisfying answer.

By the Book

Amazing grace! how sweet the sound,
That sav'd a wretch like me!
I once was lost, but now am found,
Was blind, but now I see.
> —John Newton, repentant slave trader (1725–1807)[1]

■ ■ ■

The devil doesn't care which side of the horse we fall off of, as long as we don't stay in the saddle.
> —Martin Luther, church reformer (1483–1586)[2]

■ ■ ■

"I have not spoken in secret,
    from somewhere in a land of darkness;
I have not said to Jacob's descendants,
    'Seek me in vain.'
I, the LORD, speak the truth;
    I declare what is right."
> —Isaiah 45:19

If you don't believe me, I would encourage you to dig deeply into the Bible and the many great books that have been written on the subject of Christian apologetics (see Appendix IV).

And, here's a bit of food for thought: While I haven't given you all the answers here, I have encouraged you to dig deeply. Do you honestly think I would be giving you this advice if I thought that by following it you would turn *away* from faith?

That just doesn't make sense at all!

III. A Biblical Worldview

But I must confess that I don't want you to be a mere spiritual survivor—someone whose faith was not destroyed by college. I don't want you to just survive, but to thrive! And if you've stuck with me this far, I'm guessing that you want that for yourself, too. That's why I want to introduce the idea of a biblical worldview.

What is a worldview? According to James Sire, a worldview is a "set of assumptions . . . about the basic makeup of the world." Sire, in

---

A Word from the Faculty

It is imperative that Christian students enter college well prepared to face attacks to both the historical facts as well as the philosophical basis of Christianity. Even more important, Christians must keep current on these matters. But rest assured that since you know the Truth, you have nothing to fear as you continue to search for truth.

—*David Beck, Ph.D., professor of philosophy*
at Liberty University, Virginia

his marvelous book *The Universe Next Door*, says that those assumptions may be "true, partially true, or entirely false." He also says that we cannot avoid having these assumptions. We hold them "consciously or subconsciously, consistently or inconsistently."[3] Our worldview is like a pair of glasses through which we view everything. If these glasses are tinted, then our view of the world is flawed. If the glasses are clear, so is our view of the world.

Your worldview lens

Let me share a story that will help you see how powerful a worldview can be. It is probably apocryphal—that is, it is one that has never been fully confirmed with historical evidence—but it does point to an important truth. The great explorer Magellan stopped on the western coast of South America during his sixteenth-century circumnavigation of the world. He anchored his ship in the harbor and came ashore in smaller vessels. The native people were hospitable and intelligent, and before too many days had passed the two peoples could communicate fairly effectively. At some point in the interaction, the South Americans were able to ask two questions. First, how did the Europeans travel so far across the ocean in the small boats they came ashore in, boats that were like their own and that they knew would not handle the ocean storms. Second, they wanted to know if the explorers had been to the new "island" they now saw in their harbor.

The South Americans had never seen a boat as large as Magellan's ship. They could not conceive of such a craft being built and sailed by human hands. Their assumptions were so strong that it took a good bit of explaining before they understood that this large ship was not an island, but the vessel on which they sailed, and these small boats were stowed on the ship and used only for coming ashore.[4]

So it is with our worldviews. Worldviews are strong lenses through which we see and interpret reality. If the lenses are flawed, then our understanding of reality is flawed. Think of it like this: If the lenses in your glasses are tinted, you will never know the true color of things. If the lenses magnify things, you will not know their true size. Or, to extend the analogy further, imagine that you tried to find out how large a room was by using a flashlight rather than by turning on the floodlights. Or imagine that the only light you ever used was a black light or a strobe light. Your view of what is going on around you would be radically altered.

In a way, that's what college is like. You'll be surrounded by people who have wildly divergent views of the world. Some of these views may have an element of truth in them, and because of that, it may be hard to see that the larger view is actually false. So let's take a look at some of these "lenses" through which people look at the world:

- naturalistic lens: an evolutionary worldview; most academic disciplines are reinterpreted from this perspective
- liberal theological lens: religions, like social customs, simply evolved and are man's attempts at creating order
- political lens: through socialism or liberalism, man can usher in utopia, and must!

Overheard in the Student Lounge

Christian students should learn to build relationships with people outside their regular scope of friends. We are called to reach out, to minister. It may seem hard to talk with people you don't know, but you can learn to do it. That's the way to enlarge your view of the world. Look outside your little corner of the world.

—Ester C., Brazil

The atheistic lens of a few decades ago has been replaced with an intensely spiritual one. But the god of modern spirituality is

- antisupernatural;
- impersonal;
- nonmoral;
- nonjudgmental

The true spiritual lens uses Truth, not just feelings, to help you find your way through life's challenges.

EVERYTEEN Joel

Joel would not give in to the idea that all religions were right. He knew he had to decide if his beliefs were based on more than being born into a Christian family.

By the third week of class, Joel was spending almost as much time studying about the validity of the Bible as he was for the rest of his classes. His parents ordered a few books about Jesus from Amazon.com and had them shipped to him. As soon as they arrived, Joel began poring over them. He also began a series of e-mails with the InterVarsity Christian Fellowship leaders on campus. In those messages, Joel asked questions about how the books of the Bible were selected and how Christians knew the words of Jesus were accurately written down and not just made up by the disciples or corrupted hundreds of years later.

What he learned surprised him and solidified his biblical worldview.

■   ■   ■

Whatever lens you now have filtering your worldview, make it a lifetime goal to see everything through the lens of biblical truth. As you mature spiritually, your view will change, becoming clearer and crisper;

colors and textures you never dreamed of will begin to appear. You'll start seeing God in places He seemed hidden before. It's as if you'll be looking through a kaleidoscope, and suddenly a Rembrandt master-piece comes into focus. God's handiwork and purpose in the world are evident for everyone who is willing to look for them. They may be shrouded at many colleges and universities, but if you know what you're looking for, you'll find truth even in the darkest of places.

Chapter 3

Emotional Stability

The LORD is a refuge for the oppressed,
a **strong**hold in times of trouble.

—*Psalm 9:9*

College is a time of emotional highs and lows. You may grieve leaving home, even if you couldn't wait to get out! These highs and lows are so powerful that they can blow you off course in life, but if you maintain an even keel and use these highs and lows to your advantage, they can also be a powerful force, propelling you toward God's highest and best for your life.

EVERYTEEN Megan

Remember Megan? She was the young woman with great intellectual potential. You may recall that she was the salutatorian of her large senior class, and was accepted at many colleges.

Because Megan had a broad range of interests, she selected a large state school that would give her a wide variety of academic choices. Being on a large campus, though, created a great loneliness in Megan. She went from being at the top of her high school class and many a teacher's favorite to college where she was just one more face in a crowd. She had trouble finding classes that fit her. The tough classes were stimulating, but she had to work hard just to make B's, something she was not used to. And she felt as if she was wasting her time in the easier classes.

For Megan, however, the increased pressures of college plus the high expectations she put on herself left her emotionally drained. She noticed another young man who was also taking some of the tough classes she was taking. They joined a chemistry study group together and started going to and from class together. Megan knew he was not the one for her. He was not, after all, even a Christian. But she felt a bit less lonely when he was around. He was smart and seemed to know where he was going in life. He may not have been a Christian, but he was a nice guy who treated Megan with respect. She knew lots of Christian guys who behaved much worse.

Emotional traps

Megan didn't know it, but she was about to fall into an emotional trap.

Traps are interesting devices. Consider a mousetrap or some other animal trap. Or a speed trap, those spots on the highway where the speed limit suddenly drops by 20 or more miles per hour, and you're caught—stuck with a costly speeding ticket.

Sure, some of these traps are completely hidden and catch their prey by surprise. But more often than not, we know the traps are there. I grew up on a farm and saw many animals trapped. Most of the time the animal is suspicious. It circles the trap. It sniffs. It knows something is wrong, but it also sees the bait. Its desire for the bait overwhelms its natural caution or the wisdom of experience.

So it is with emotional traps. Megan knew she was in dangerous territory but not strong enough to resist the temptation. But before we find out what happened to her, let's look at some common emotional traps you are likely to encounter.

Social traps

The need to belong is a strong force. It is also a God-given desire. God did not make us to be lone rangers. According to His plan, we are born into families, which is our first social network. Our church is, or should be, an extension of our family—not replacing the family, but supporting it. When we reject God's plan for getting our social needs met and replace His plan with another, then this need to belong becomes a trap.

Illegal drugs

Drugs can be a particularly destructive trap. Illegal drugs and many prescription drugs almost always have an addictive physiological component. Because of that, even a strong desire to quit is sometimes not enough. No drug addict ever said to himself, "Today, I'm going to become a drug addict and see how badly I can screw up my life." No,

A Word from the Faculty

The most potent antidote to loneliness for the Christian is genuine Christian fellowship. Look for campus Christian groups and participate actively in them. If none are available, contact the chaplain or office of religious life and ask the person in charge if there are faculty members or professional staff on campus who identify themselves as evangelical Christians. These folks usually welcome Christian students and can provide a great deal of encouragement, as well as direction in finding local congregations that can meet your spiritual and social needs.

—*Michael Murray, Ph.D., professor and chairman of philosophy department, Franklin and Marshall College, Pennsylvania*

drug use never begins that way. Drug use almost always begins because of an emotional pain or need. It could be the desire to fit in with a group or the desire to dull an emotional hurt. Drug use is never the problem; it is a symptom of the problem.

If you fall into the trap of illegal drug addiction, you can also quickly develop legal problems that can cripple you for the rest of your life.

Alcohol

The same is true of alcohol. The major difference between alcohol and drugs is that for many college students alcohol is both legal and—in most circles—socially acceptable.

Promiscuity

Statistics indicate that many young people have their first sexual encounters while in college. Why? Did they suddenly lose their moral bearings? Possibly, but a more significant reason is simply that the opportunity presented itself. If you are lonely and not under the watchful eye of parents, you might do things you wouldn't otherwise do. But make no mistake: Premarital sexual activity, regardless of the motivation, can have lifelong consequences. Besides the obvious possibilities of disease and pregnancy, there is the too-often underappreciated reality that when you give yourself to someone sexually, you also give your heart to him or her, whether you want to or not. Sexual promiscuity is not itself the problem but is a symptom of a deeper spiritual and emotional problem.

Materialism

One of the most socially acceptable addictions in our society, even among Christians, is the trap of materialism. Materialism is acceptable because its symptoms often look like virtues, not vices. People pursuing materialism are often smart and disciplined. They are hard workers and thrifty. Sometimes they even give large sums of money—or their time—to Christian work. But Jesus reserved some of His most scathing criticism for the rich. He said that it is harder for a rich man to enter heaven than it is for a camel to go through the eye of a needle. Matthew 6:24 tells us that we cannot serve two masters; we cannot serve both "God and Money."

Alex on His Soapbox

Getting ready for college involves more than just tuition and fees.

The average incoming freshman will spend about $1,200 in preparation for that first semester. In a survey of more than 6,000 students, the National Retail Federation determined that students leaving for college annually spend a staggering $3.6 billion (yes, billion) on dorm room décor. But in heading for school, remember that a positive college experience is not about how much "bling you bring."[1]

I beg each of you reading this book right now—watch out for the dangers of credit card debt. Credit card companies actively recruit on campus, and to young students who may never have had a credit card before, it feels like "free" money whenever you whip out the plastic to pay. It's easy to rack up huge debts this way, and what seemed "free" before becomes anything but as creditors start to call and your credit rating is ruined.

How Close to the Edge Do You Want to Get?

My guess is that as you read my short descriptions of these emotional traps, you were asking yourself questions about each one of them. "Is Alex saying that I shouldn't get a good job and make money?" Or, "Are cigarettes a drug?" Or, "If I kiss my girlfriend, is that being promiscuous?"

These may not have been *your* questions, but I'm guessing that you had a few of your own. And, to be honest, these questions are not bad ones. For example, the Bible tells us that riches and power can be deceptive and destructive. But it also tells us, "If a man will not work, he shall not eat" (2 Thessalonians 3:10). Jesus tells us in Luke 10:7 that "the worker deserves his wages." That means, in part, it is good to work for money.

No, these questions are not all black and white. Part of growing to full maturity as a Christian is wrestling deeply with Scripture—and your own motives—to come to the place where you believe God would have you.

But as you do so, consider the story of the king whose coachman, after years of honorable service, was being granted a pension and retirement. The king sent word out that the best coachmen in the land should gather at his castle for a competition to see who would get the job of driving for the king. The king ultimately narrowed the competitors down to two, and he gave them a final test: drive the king's coach on the most treacherous road in the kingdom and return safely.

Each coachman took off, and soon one was far in the lead. He careened around each turn in the road. He sprayed rocks off steep cliffs, and he arrived back at the castle well ahead of his competitor. But, to the consternation of the fast but reckless coachman and to the surprise of many in the kingdom, the king chose the coachman who made the trip slowly and carefully. When the disappointed coachman asked why he was not chosen, the king answered, "Your daring and skill are great, but you forgot that it would be your king and your queen and their children who would be riding in the coach."

I share that story to ask this question: How close to the edge of the cliff do you want to get? We should never forget that we live our lives to bring glory to our king, the King of kings. Our goal should not be to see how close to these emotional traps we can get without getting caught—but how far away we can remain!

Making Major Life Decisions

One of the great outdoor adventures of the twentieth century was the conquering of Mount Everest. Since it was first climbed by Sir Edmund Hillary and his Sherpa guide, Tenzing Norgay, hundreds of others have reached the summit—but more than a hundred have also perished in the attempt.

Overheard in the Student Lounge

Freshmen should know that it is a lot easier to make friends in the first few weeks of school than at any other time. You need to take advantage of the fact that every freshman on campus will be looking for friends. Do not sit in your room chatting with high school friends on AIM— that will only cripple any hope of a social life. Make an honest effort to meet people. This will be one of the easiest times in your life to do so. Having a good group of friends will make your entire college experience easier and more fun.

—*Anonymous*

What's surprising is most of the people who have died on Everest died not on the ascent but on the descent. Experts say there are two reasons for this. First, most people who climb Everest have made the summit the object of an almost obsessive compulsion for which they have been preparing for months and even years. The whole focus is on getting to the top, and once they get to the top, they let their guard down, becoming sloppy and careless. They then make a mistake that costs them their lives.

The second reason people die on the descent is they get so close to the summit they can't bear to see it slip away. They push ahead even though their reserves of energy have been thoroughly depleted, leaving them with nothing for the descent.

That's why experienced Everest climbers have developed what is called "the 2 P.M. Rule." It is a simple rule experienced climbers know and follow: At 2 P.M., no matter where you are, turn back. Don't think about it; just turn back! The 2 P.M. Rule was designed because when you've been climbing for days or weeks and you're in the oxygen-starved atmosphere near the summit of the peak, you'll make bad decisions. The 2 P.M. Rule leaves no room for bad judgment.

I am just as susceptible as you are to all of the emotional traps I have outlined here. That is why I follow a simple rule like The 2 P.M. Rule. It has kept me and will keep you out of trouble. It will prevent you from finding yourself in situations where your only options are bad ones: Don't make any major life decisions if you're *Hungry, Angry, Lonely,* or *Tired.* These four words form a simple acronym: HALT.

Hungry

Maybe you've heard the saying you shouldn't buy groceries when you're hungry. You'll buy what you're hungry for and not necessarily what you need. And you won't look at the price. You'll pay too much for everything. If you're emotionally hungry—for affection, attention, or companionship—you'll also pay too much. When you're emotionally hungry, get fed from the people who have fed you in the past: family, old and trusted friends, Scripture, prayer, and church. If you're *still* hungry afterward, perhaps God is nudging you in a new direction, but proceed with wisdom and care.

Angry

Police investigators will tell you the overwhelming majority of murders are committed by people who know their victims. Often the murderer and the victim are family members. In a flash of anger, one of them does something that has an eternal consequence for both of them. It is my sincere hope and prayer that you will never be angry enough at anyone to commit murder, but I use this example to suggest that if anger is powerful enough to get otherwise reasonable people to commit murder, surely it can also motivate many lesser but also destructive actions. When you're angry, avoid major decisions. Sit down. Cool off. Do whatever you do to calm down. Then think through your options.

Lonely

A strong factor determining whether two people will get married is geography. In other words, you have relationships with those around you. Woody Allen said it another way: "Eighty percent of success is just showing up."[2] That's why making a major life decision, especially about relationships, is dangerous when you're lonely. You're likely to go with what is nearest at hand, what is easiest and most accessible, and not necessarily what is best for you.

Tired

Warren Smith (my friend who helped me write this book) has gone on many long-distance backpacking trips. He even hiked the

Appalachian Trail, a 2,000-mile path that runs from Maine to Georgia. I once asked him if he used the shelters strategically located along the path. He replied, "Yes, I've used them. But if I'm tired enough, I can plop down just about anywhere." He said that one night he was so tired he slept in the middle of the trail, and he slept so soundly that he didn't hear it begin to rain. When he finally woke up, his sleeping bag was a muddy mess that took nearly a week to dry out. He was

By the Book

"And surely I am with you always, to the very end of the age."
—*Jesus (Matthew 28:20)*

■ ■ ■

Language . . . has created the word "loneliness" to express the pain of being alone. And it has created the word "solitude" to express the glory of being alone.
—*Paul Tillich, American theologian (1886–1965)*[3]

■ ■ ■

Trust in the LORD and do good;
    dwell in the land and enjoy safe pasture.
Delight yourself in the LORD
    and he will give you the desires of your heart.
Commit your way to the LORD;
    trust in him and he will do this:
He will make your righteousness shine like the dawn,
    the justice of your cause like the noonday sun.
—*Psalm 37:3-6*

never able to get it clean again. When you're tired, you'll make compromises you wouldn't otherwise make. You'll look for the shortcut or the easy way. And the easy way is rarely the best way.

EVERYTEEN Megan

So what happened to Megan? She fell into several of these traps. Because she was lonely, she slowly started giving her heart to a young man who was not a Christian—but who was near at hand. As their relationship became more intimate emotionally, it became difficult for Megan to back out of the relationship. She ended up putting herself in a situation that had no good solution; she had set herself up for pain if she stayed in the relationship or if she left. Unfortunately, her loneliness left her so depressed that she didn't have the energy to make a decision. So she began to emotionally coast, taking the path of least resistance.

■   ■   ■

Don't fall into the same trap. Your first months in college will be times of emotional highs and lows. Be aware of what is happening. Enjoy the ride as much as you can. The highs and lows, the ups and downs. But never forget the sign they place on the roller coaster as it's leaving the station: "Keep your arms and legs inside the car at all times!"

During these highs and lows, guard your mind and your heart, and when you get back to the station, that will be soon enough to decide what attraction you'll ride next!

Chapter 4

Physical Disciplines

Be **strong** and do not give up,
for your work will be rewarded.

—*2 Chronicles 15:7*

One of the best illustrations I've seen on the value of self-discipline comes from *The Karate Kid.* This movie was popular when I was in high school. In fact, *Entertainment Weekly* named it number 31 on its list of the 50 best high school films of all time.[1] The story follows a skinny kid named Danny LaRusso (played by Ralph Macchio) who wanted to learn karate so he could stand up to the bullies in his school. Mr. Miyagi (played by Pat Morita) chose to help Danny learn karate, but Mr. Miyagi wanted his student to learn to love karate and to develop mastery over his life—not to merely seek revenge. Mr. Miyagi's first lesson was for Danny to spend an entire day waxing Mr. Miyagi's collection of vintage cars. Mr. Miyagi was very specific about the hand motions Danny had to use. "Wax on, wax off," Mr. Miyagi said, demonstrating the hand motions.

Danny reluctantly complied, meticulously waxing Mr. Miyagi's cars all day until he had had it. Next he spent a day sanding floors, then two days painting the fence and the house. All of these tasks were done with controlled arm movements as specified by Mr. Miyagi.

Danny finally went back to Mr. Miyagi and, with what energy he had left, complained bitterly that this "wax on, wax off" nonsense had nothing to do with becoming a karate master.[2]

Mr. Miyagi then showed Danny the purpose of the waxing by attempting some quick karate chops directed at Danny. Instinctively, Danny defended himself using the same "wax on, wax off" hand motions he had learned waxing the cars. Mr. Miyagi got his cars waxed, Danny had mastered vital karate skills, and Danny's love and respect for Mr. Miyagi deepened.

I certainly do not want to compare Mr. Miyagi to God, but I will compare Danny to you and to me. Physical disciplines can do more than build our physical strength. They can have a positive impact on our emotional, intellectual, and spiritual lives.

In chapter 2 we learned that we are not our own. All of creation, which includes you and me, belongs to God. We are God's property, and we are stewards of God's property. If you want to enter college with a prepared heart, you must have the self-control to manage your time and your body. A heart that does not have the ability to act and control the rest of the body is ineffective at best and in the worst cases can lead to tragedy.

Overheard in the Student Lounge

Incoming freshmen should know that they will be challenged in every aspect of life, more so than they ever were in high school. College will test you morally, intellectually, and spiritually. Succeeding in college will even test you physically—I am literally talking about sleep deprivation!

—*Anonymous*

Sharing God's Priorities

I know plenty of people who tend to spiritualize everything in regard to time management; they think everything good will just flow naturally from a passion for God. "Just love God and the rest will follow," they say. "You won't have to *make* yourself have a quiet time, set aside time to study the Bible, or find a new church in your college town. No, you will *want* to do all of these things. And if you're struggling with any of these things, it's because you just don't love God enough!"

This tendency to spiritualize things when it comes to taking action regarding our priorities has some truth in it. But it's only part of the truth.

If some Christians tend to spiritualize things, others tend to prioritize things. Maybe you've seen people like this. They have their to-do lists. They put everything on a calendar. They're hyperorganized, überstructured. They carry around laptops, cell phones, Day-Timers, all manner of high-tech devices. Even in high school you probably ran into people like this, and you may have even admired them. They made good grades, played sports, and were involved in all kinds of extracurricular activities. Their lives were planned from before sunrise until after their heads hit the pillow.

So what's wrong with that? Nothing . . . and everything. A hyperfrenetic and organized life is socially acceptable. People who live this way are often successful and look happy. But I've observed that a lot of people who engage in lives like this reach a meltdown point. If it happens early, they discover they've gone through college and don't have any significant friends or relationships. If it goes on too long—say 20 years—they suddenly realize they hate their jobs. They discover that for all their achievements and planning, they didn't put time on the schedule for their spouses or children, and now they've lost them or are on the verge of losing them.

Part of becoming an adult is developing the ability to take the long view of life. It's called delayed gratification. And nowhere is taking the long view more important than in the matters of time management and self-control.

To better explore this idea, let's look at EVERYTEENS Adam and Erin to see how they're doing.

EVERYTEENS Adam and Erin

Adam was the natural leader. People gravitated toward him. Things came easily for him—too easily. In high school Adam never really developed the kind of discipline he needed for college. Sure he did well in high school, but it was only because his parents, teachers, and coaches structured and monitored his activities. At college no one was there to tell him what to do and when to do it, so Adam quickly fell into bad habits in the free and easy atmosphere of the dorms.

During high school, his parents and friends expected Adam to go to youth group and church. So he did and had a good time, as was his nature. But in college, Adam spent his time partying, going to bed late and getting up late, eating irregularly, and generally just squandering his time socializing or recovering from socializing. While he still cared about God, his commitment wasn't strong enough to rein in his social drives.

Because Adam didn't get wasted, none of his friends noticed he was getting in trouble and couldn't manage the rigorous freshman core classes. After the first semester, he was on academic probation.

■   ■   ■

Erin, the new Christian, was having some troubles, too. Keeping in shape for water polo meant three hours in the pool a day, minimum.

The workouts were harder than anything she'd imagined; had she mistakenly signed up for the marines or something? She was also checking into every single Christian club on campus, looking for the perfect group. She did her devotions every day, but sometimes it felt as if she were just going through the motions. Her physics class was difficult, and the lab times took a big chunk of her day. She had to hire a tutor to keep her grade up. Some days she literally didn't have time to make it back to the dorms for dinner, so she would eat peanut butter instead. She'd drop into bed exhausted at night, ignoring dozens of e-mails from her high school friends that she had hoped to answer in her spare time, a concept that was becoming nothing but a fading memory, as was the luxury of clean laundry.

Take the High Road

Adam was taking the easy road—he just did what he wanted to do when he wanted to. Erin had everything organized, but she still wasn't in control of her life. In some ways, the person who spiritualizes everything is the person who sees a mountain in front of him but lacks the

A Word from the Faculty

Of the students who succeed, I would say that one attribute that they must have is resilience. You have to have the ability to say, "Okay, today didn't go so well, but tomorrow I will do better." You must keep going, one step at a time. Problems will come, but you keep going, one day at a time.

—*Alayne Zimmerly, Ph.D., professor of education,*
University of Arkansas

discipline to climb it. He takes the road to the right—downhill and downstream, thinking he's headed for the clear blue ocean but ending up in a spiritual swamp. This was Adam's approach. He really thought that if he just followed his heart, God would work everything out for him. Unfortunately, his heart was off the true path, and it led him into academic trouble.

But the person who prioritizes everything is also in danger. When the spiritualizer turns in one direction, the prioritizer turns in the opposite direction. He is disciplined, but merciless and dogmatic. For the prioritizer, switchback upon switchback marks the road ahead. He spends most of his time going back and forth and very little time actually going up. This is what Erin was doing. She had every minute of her day scheduled, and she rarely had time for anything significant. She was working hard enough, but she wasn't getting any closer to where she really wanted to be, which was closer to Jesus.

Neither Adam nor Erin was headed on the right path.

So what does the right path look like? Here are some signposts that will help you know you are on the right road as you climb.

Time Management

You've heard all the clichés about time: "Time is the only nonrenewable resource." "A stitch in time saves nine." "If only I had more time." That's the tragic lament of students as they face an exam, football coaches as they face the final seconds of the game, and dissatisfied old people as they look back on their lives.

Time is indeed our most precious resource and one of humankind's most enduring preoccupations. In fact, the concept of time is also an important theme in Scripture. Here are just a few verses that refer to time:

- [Redeem] the time, because the days are evil. (Ephesians 5:16, KJV)
- A little sleep, a little slumber, a little folding of the hands to rest—and poverty will come on you like a bandit and scarcity like an armed man. (Proverbs 6:10-11)
- No one knows about that day or hour [of the Lord's return]. (Matthew 24:36)

Managing our time in a way that is pleasing to God is much more than just getting organized and adhering to a schedule, as Erin was trying to do. It involves being aware of God's calling on your life and being sensitive to the opportunities God is placing before you. But getting organized is a good place to start, so let's talk about that first.

Keeping a calendar—the basics

If you are not already consistently writing things on a calendar, begin to develop that habit from the first day you enter college. I recommend a calendar that has plenty of space for each day, space that will allow you to plan your day hour by hour. Some calendars even give you the ability to schedule 15-minute intervals.

When you get your calendar, mark all the commitments and appointments you know about. Use a pencil, because things are sure to change! Here's a quick guide to make sure that you cover the basics:

Recurring commitments. You already know that you need to attend class every day. Block out those times. You will want to eat and sleep every day. Write those things in your calendar, too! Are you on a sports team, in a club or Christian group? Do you have a regular Bible study? Putting these recurring, nondiscretionary commitments on your calendar first will make it much more likely that you'll keep your priorities in order and that you'll meet your basic obligations to others and to yourself.

Study time. There are as many different study habits as there are people, but the most successful students develop a rigorous study routine. That's why I strongly recommend that you schedule two hours of study time each week for every one hour you spend in class—and write these times in your calendar, too! You may discover that this formula doesn't fit you exactly, but my experience is that it will be close. The worst that can happen if you follow this formula in your first few months of college is that it will be impossible for you to get too far behind.

Recurring discretionary commitments. When you have scheduled all your nondiscretionary commitments and study time, take a look at your calendar. What's left is free time. But it's not really free, because everything you do during that time has a cost; it is what economists call an opportunity cost. In other words, you can surf around on the Internet or play a video game during your free time, but during that time you cannot exercise or get in an extra hour of study so you can go to the football game on Saturday. Everything you do has a cost.

That's why I also strongly recommend that you have some priorities and goals and that you write them into your schedule, too. An obvious one is exercise. You might have a hobby you want to pursue or a skill you want to develop or maintain. Schedule it! Write it down on your calendar. Turn your dreams into goals and your goals into items on your schedule. Before long, you'll notice that your dreams are slowly coming true.

Margin time. Without time reserves in your life, you risk emotional, financial, spiritual, and physical breakdowns. Perhaps it would be better if you didn't have to schedule margins into your life. But having rest times because you schedule them is better than not having rest times at all.

Trading time. You may be thinking, *But, Alex, I don't want to be a slave to this calendar.* I don't want you to be a slave, either. More important, God doesn't want you to be a slave to any man or any man-made system. Scripture even has something explicit to say about this: "It is for freedom that Christ has set us free" (Galatians 5:1). But by writing *everything* down in your calendar, including margin time, you can have mastery over your schedule. Surprises and interruptions are diminished. And you can then move beyond the basics of time management to an advanced skill, "trading time."

Let's say you're studying. You're one hour into a two-hour block of study time, and then you have an hour of exercise scheduled before supper. And because you've scheduled your studying and stuck to your schedule, you know that your evening is free. You've got it all planned out! But there's knock on your door, and there's a friend with a distraught look on her face. She wants to talk. Because you have mastery over your schedule, you don't have to brush off your friend because you're in panic study mode. You can say to your friend, "Come on in. Let's talk." And you can truly listen rather than have one part of your mind worried about your studying or whether you're going to get your exercise in today. Because you know what you need to do, and you have margin time built in to your schedule, you can trade time between the blocks.

Physical Health

It is helpful to ask what God has to say about our physical bodies and our physical health. In Genesis 1:10, 12, and 25, God declared His creation "good." In Genesis 1:31 the Bible goes even further by calling the man God had created "very good." Paul's letter to the Ephesians takes things one step further. He wrote, "We are God's workmanship" (2:10).

So God made the physical world, and He made us as the masterpiece of His creation. So doesn't it make sense that what God values, we should value too?

There is a second foundational truth: The way we treat our bodies is an act of worship. Romans 12:1 states this truth explicitly: "Therefore, I urge you, brothers, in view of God's mercy, to offer your bodies as living sacrifices, holy and pleasing to God—this is your spiritual act of worship."

Scripture says that your body is "a temple of the Holy Spirit" (1 Corinthians 6:19). For the Christian, that reality alone should cause us to take the care of our body seriously.

Let's discuss some health issues that are particularly relevant to you as you enter college.

The freshman 15

The "freshman 15" are those extra unwanted pounds that result when you combine the freedom to do what you want with an all-you-can-eat cafeteria and the occasional late-night pizza.

There are emotional factors that go into our relationship with food. It is beyond the scope of this book to have an in-depth discussion of bulimia, anorexia, and other eating disorders, which affect women in overwhelmingly disproportionate numbers. But I do want to observe that experts in these maladies are unanimous on this point: There are emotional and spiritual dimensions to our physical health. That said, go research for tips on keeping weight off. (It only gets more difficult as you get older.)

Exercise

So much has been written about physical exercise that I don't want to spend a lot of time on it here. Muscle and health magazines, exercise infomercials, health clubs, and sports merchandise companies are now dominant parts of pop culture. We have become an exercise-obsessed society.

But I would like to observe that this obsession is something different from a truly godly discipline. The overriding concern for the Christian when it comes to exercise should be this consideration: Is it making me fit for long-term service to God? The goal of exercise is not to look sexy in a pair of jeans or to be able to show off your six-pack abs at the swimming pool. The goal of exercise is to make you fit for service in the army of the King!

Alcohol and drugs

My guess is that you've heard so many lectures about alcohol and drugs over the years that you can barely stand the possibility of one more. To be honest, I've talked about this issue so many times, I can barely stand to do it once more. Most such talks amount to little more

Alex on His Soapbox

Your mom was right. There is a connection between eating a good breakfast and your ability to perform well throughout the day. Your ability to think and function is affected by the level of sugar in the blood. Blood glucose levels are dependent on how many calories, carbs, and proteins you ingest. All of this determines how much blood goes to the brain (you know, that thing you think with), which will not function correctly without enough glucose. So, optimum physical and intellectual performance, especially in the morning hours, is partly contingent on a good breakfast. Just go to bed so that you can be up in plenty of time for breakfast!

than a lot of statistics about how many people are using drugs, a lot of statistics and stories about how destructive they are, and an admonition not to drink or do drugs.

And yet, people still drink alcohol and do drugs.

Why? **Why? WHY?**

I think it's because alcohol and drugs really do help some people—at least temporarily. Some shy people who want to be more outgoing really do become less inhibited when they drink alcohol. Some lonely and depressed people who take certain drugs really do feel better.

But at what cost?

There is an old joke that tells of two policemen looking at a dead body on the sidewalk in front of a tall building. The rookie policeman asks, "Did he die from the fall?" The veteran policeman answers, "No, he died from the sudden stop at the end."

Indeed, if it weren't for that sudden stop at the end, more of us might be tempted to jump off of buildings for the thrill of it!

For too many people, the thrill and temporary good feelings created by alcohol and drugs result in a sudden stop from which they might never recover. But rather than scare you out of using drugs and alcohol, let me suggest to you that alcohol and drugs are not the problem; they are a symptom of the problem. Abuse of alcohol and drugs are the symptoms of an emotionally and spiritually empty life.

So here's my lecture about alcohol and drugs: Stay away from drugs, period. They are expensive, they are bad for you, and they are illegal.

There are some Christians who believe that alcohol, if not abused, is allowed by Scripture. Personally, I abstain altogether and would encourage any and all to follow this path. But even if you believe that alcohol is allowable, why not abstain from it during the time you're in college as a kind of "fast" or spiritual discipline?

The spiritual benefits from even this kind of limited fasting are profound, and you'll discover that the desires you thought the alcohol fulfilled will be more than met by the spiritual, physical, and emotional strength you'll develop.

The gift of sex

Sex is one of God's greatest gifts to humankind and a powerful force that shapes individuals, families, and entire cultures. But consider nitroglycerine. It is also an enormously powerful force. It can make drag racers go fast. It can blast through rock so that tunnels, bridges, and skyscrapers can be built. It can be an enormous force for good.

By the Book

All successful people have the habit of doing the things failures don't like to do. They don't like doing them either, necessarily. But their disliking is subordinated to the strength of their purpose.[3]

—Albert E. Grays

■ ■ ■

And God is able to make all grace abound to you, so that in all things at all times, having all that you need, you will abound in every good work.

—2 Corinthians 9:8

■ ■ ■

Far and away the best prize that life offers is to work hard at work worth doing.

—Theodore Roosevelt, 26th U.S. president (1858–1919)[4]

But uncontrolled, or in the hands of evil or incompetent people, it can be an enormously destructive force.

You may be thinking, *Okay, fine, Alex, I'm all for that. I would also like to evangelize the world and cure world hunger. Don't tell me what to do; tell me how to do it.* Said another way, how do you keep that nitro in the bottle until it is the good and proper time for its use?

If you focus on the sacrifice and abstinence, you probably won't have the strength to remain celibate indefinitely. But if you understand that knowing God in a deeper and richer way is one of the results of abstaining from extramarital activity, then, as Jesus said, His "yoke is easy and [his] burden is light" (Matthew 11:30).

Church and parachurch activities

One of the things I love about my life and work is the fact that I get to travel around the country and speak in churches and on college campuses. Several years ago during a tour of "50 States in 50 Days," I preached in a different church, in a different state, every day, until I preached in every state. Over the years I have met thousands of Christian leaders, from all levels of ministry, some with famous names you would know, others whose names are only well-known in heaven because of their years of faithful service to God. The overwhelming majority of them tell me their college years were pivotal in both their decision to follow Jesus and in their decision to make ministry their full-time career. College was when they knew clearly God's calling on their lives. Get involved in a church or parachurch ministry quickly!

EVERYTEENS Adam and Erin

Erin flew home for winter break and slept the entire time. Her mother dragged her to a doctor, who said she had mono. She went back to school with some medication and had to cut out her training for water polo and most of her church activities. She did keep going to a dorm Bible study for women because it was close and didn't take much preparation time. There she began to make some good friends. Because her body made her slow down and she couldn't keep the pace she had when she first arrived, her life unexpectedly mellowed to a better balance. She was more satisfied with doing less.

■　■　■

Don't wait until you are over your limits or in a crisis to do something about your schedule, physical habits, sexual relationships, or addiction(s). Be honest with yourself and with God. Determine some boundaries ahead of time and do something about it if you cross one. If Adam had gone to his academic adviser or pastor after he got his second D on a test, he might have curtailed his social life and had an overall better first semester. Or if he had decided ahead of time that two nights out per week was enough socializing, he probably would have been okay. Seek help early if you need it. Putting out a small fire with a fire extinguisher is a lot easier than waiting to put out a full blaze and needing to call 911.

Part 2

An Unshakable Faith

Be on your guard; stand firm in the faith; . . . be **strong**.
—*1 Corinthians 16:13*

Robert Wilson was a gifted scholar. By the time he left Princeton at age 20, he could read the New Testament in nine languages. But being smart didn't make his academic road easy. In college, Robert ran into a lot of scholars who pooh-poohed Christianity and were actively seeking to discredit the Bible.

In fact, while Robert was earning his undergraduate and doctorate degrees, the academic climate increasingly turned against Christianity. Most of the leading scholars and professors Robert knew taught that the Bible was false and that Christianity was outdated. It grieved Robert to hear influential leaders deliver lectures actually ridiculing Jesus and driving students to question the Bible.

"Yeah, so what?" you might want to say. "That happens to me every single day in high school." But this wasn't recent history; it was 1876. The American Civil War had been over for only 11 years. Back then, the Ten Commandments were still on the walls of courthouses, and first-graders learned to read "*A* is for Adam." Christianity was part of mainstream culture, and most people accepted Scripture at face value.

But the academic community was bucking that culture and trying to pitch out the Bible. Robert knew that the charges of the doubters should be answered. Most of all, he knew that the accusations of the skeptical scholars *could be answered.*

Robert decided to invest his entire academic future and professional life to the study of the Bible. Few have ever studied the Bible and ancient languages to the degree that Robert did. Maybe no one.

But Robert didn't set out to become one of the greatest scholars who ever lived. It just happened. Things like that do when you *master* 45 languages.

Academic Overkill?

Before I finish the story of Robert, let me say a few things. You probably know by now that I think Christians should have a solid understanding of their faith. You wouldn't be reading this book unless you
believed that on some level or another. I believe that the continual
development of one's heart *and* mind are also a duty.

But I don't want to put you on a guilt trip. Not everyone can be
a superintellect like Robert. You're not a second-class Christian if you
don't learn Hebrew, Greek, Aramaic, and Syriac. To put this in perspective, when I graduated from college, I knew English and just
enough Spanish to order in a restaurant. God won't love you less if you
opt out of reading Augustine and Aquinas (though I think you'll miss
out on some great Christian insights if you do).

But our command to develop an unshakable faith comes from the
Bible itself. As a Christian, you should rise to the challenge of 1 Peter
3:15 and be adequately prepared to explain what you believe. On the
college campus, you *will* be required to defend your faith.

The intellectual accomplishments of people like Robert should
not intimidate us, but they should be an inspiration. Let's face it: God
does not give everyone the same amount of gray matter. Some people
have an intellectual edge over others. That's irrelevant. Every Christian
should do his or her best to represent the faith. Regardless of where
you go to college, the campus needs the light that you can provide!

Now, let me finish the story of Robert Wilson.

A Scholar Without Equal

At age 25, Robert decided to divide his future into three segments of
15 years each. (Yes, I know that most of us don't think this way. But
Robert was serious about being a good steward of his time.) He fig-

ured that since most of his relatives had lived to age 70, he probably would too. Given that, Robert felt that he had at least 45 more years of life. Robert observed, "The first fifteen years I would devote to the study of the languages [related to Christianity]. For the second fifteen I was going to devote myself to the study of the text of the Old Testament. And I reserved the last fifteen years for the work of writing the results of my previous studies and investigations, so as to give them to the world."[1]

Thus began decades of relentless study by one of the most meticulous scholars who ever lived. I think we can safely say that Robert possessed an unshakable faith.

While studying in Germany, Robert wrote of vulnerable students whose faith was swayed by the skepticism of the university: "The students took everything because the professor said it. I went there to study so that there would be no professor who could lay down the law for me, or say anything without my being able to investigate the evidence on which he said it."[2]

Wilson challenged the skeptics, because he knew that the facts were on the side of Christianity: "I defy any man to make an attack upon the Old Testament on the ground that I cannot investigate. I can get at the facts if they are linguistic."

Robert Wilson is often called the greatest authority on ancient Middle Eastern languages ever. The more he looked at the evidence, the greater his devotion grew to helping people understand that the Bible is trustworthy.

Over the next few decades, you may not have the time to learn 45 languages. But Robert Wilson is proof that education does not necessarily require unbelief. He left behind research that has helped many come to greater assurance and trust of the Bible.

In your own way, you can have that same unshakable faith. And you should.

Chapter 5

Academic Readiness

Be very **strong**; be careful to obey all that is
written in the Book of the Law of Moses,
without turning aside to the right or to the left.

—Joshua 23:6

Athens, Georgia, is in many ways an archetype of American college towns. The University of Georgia was carved out of the wilderness more than 200 years ago. In fact, an iron fence still encircles the old part of the campus. Today, the fence and the arch that opens onto bustling Broad Street is a famous icon and logo for the school. The arch, in particular, appears on many of the college's glossy marketing and fundraising publications. But when that iron fence was built, it was necessary to keep out ruffians and wild animals.

That's not all they wanted to keep out. One of the reasons Athens was chosen as home for the state's fledgling university was to keep out some of the more troubling influences of modernity. The early students read the classics in their original languages. Freshmen couldn't get into the school without at least basic fluency in Greek and Latin. More than a few entering freshmen—those studying "for the cloth," as they might have said then—also knew a bit of Hebrew. Athens was far removed from any significant towns so the students and their teachers could focus exclusively on higher learning.

Today, college towns like Athens are not refuges for those wanting to avoid modern popular culture; instead, they are the incubators and greenhouses of pop culture. Athens spawned the pop bands R.E.M. and the B-52s, among many others. Other college towns share those attributes: Austin, home of the University of Texas, and Charlottesville, where Thomas Jefferson founded the University of Virginia, are also thriving music towns. College towns are now where innovators take new products, new ideas—even new religions.

So step through The Arch at the University of Georgia onto Broad Street. Or maybe it's Franklin Street, which borders the University of North Carolina at Chapel Hill. Or check out the downtown pedestrian mall in Boulder, Colorado, on Halloween night—or on virtually any Saturday night. You'll see a world distinctly different from the one envisioned by college founders. I wonder what Mr. Jefferson would say if he went to a frat party at the University of Virginia. Would the hoary-headed elders of Georgia be proud of Athens now?

Let's step through The Arch. What will you see? And are you ready?

EVERYTEEN David

At the state college David attended, no one was paying any attention to him. He visited several Christian clubs, but he didn't like the leader at one, and at another the girls were all dumpy looking. The third had outdated music.

He wanted to date, but three out of three girls turned him down during the first month of school. His roommate had a job at the library and played oboe in the orchestra, so he was always gone. David spent a lot of time in his dorm room on the computer, playing games, watching YouTube, or viewing pornography.

David tried to pray, but God seemed so distant. Looking back at high school, it seemed as if his passion for God and the deeply emotional ties he had to the church had been those of a different person. When his social psychology professor said that people who claim to love Christ are following the same kind of human drive that makes people follow bands like the Grateful Dead, it made him wonder if his Christian commitment had merely been an adolescent phase. *Is there really a God?* he wondered.

No Place to Stand

So what happened to David? Every person is different, but the bottom line for most people who reject their faith is that their faith was never really that deep or mature in the first place. I know that sounds like a severe judgment, but hear me out for a moment—and let me give you a bit of an unusual analogy.

I am a guitar player. I love playing the guitar, and I love collecting guitars. Over the years I have owned more than a hundred, and I own more than a dozen today. I have also played guitar with some pretty outstanding pickers. I have even played onstage with the Beach Boys! Those moments are among the highlights of my guitar-playing career.

I have an aptitude for the guitar, but I am not wildly gifted. But because I like it, I play and practice a lot. In truth, learning to play the guitar is easy. Lots of people can master three or four chords and play many basic songs with these chords. But mastering the guitar is a long enterprise. And because I play and practice a lot, I know songs and riffs today that I did not know 10 years ago or even a year ago.

Now, what does this have to do with David and where he is headed spiritually? Everything.

You see, biblical Christianity is in some ways simple. It is the story of how much God loves the world. Even small children can remember John 3:16, which is the heart of the gospel: "For God so loved the world that he gave his one and only Son, that whoever believes in him shall not perish but have eternal life."

Yes, the gospel is so simple that even a child can understand it, but it is so deep that the smartest people working a lifetime cannot plumb its depths. Biblical Christianity answers some of the most vexing and complex questions that humankind has ever posed.

Yet what happens to most of us? We never get to those answers. We spend a few hours a month in Sunday school when we're kids, and when we get old enough to have a few tough questions that we don't know the answer to, we just assume that Christianity or the Bible is not true. That's like saying that just because you can't play the guitar like Jimi Hendrix or Phil Keaggy, it can't be done!

It is amazing to me how quickly people give up on Christianity. We make medical doctors study until they are nearly middle-aged before they are turned loose to practice medicine. And that's as it should be. The problems they are tackling are complex. Before a brain surgeon cracks into a skull, she'd better know about biology, pharmacology, and a dozen other disciplines. And not just a little bit about them, but a lot—especially if it's my skull she's cracking into!

Yet when it comes to religion, which deals with the most important and in some cases the most complicated questions humankind has devised, we will let an elementary, school understanding of God and the world dictate to us our eternal destiny. In other words, we say, "Because I don't know the answer, there must not be an answer." In no other field of human endeavor would we let that idea stand as the truth.

You may argue, "But why does following Jesus have to be so complicated? Didn't Jesus say, 'Suffer little children to come unto me, and forbid them not: for of such is the kingdom of God'?" (Luke 18:16,

KJV). C. S. Lewis has the best answer to that question; he wrote, "God wants you to have a child's heart, but a grown-up's head."[1]

So let's put on our grown-up heads and look at some of the *-isms* you will confront in college.

-Ism Defined

In the world of philosophy, politics, and theology, adding the suffix *-ism* to a word is a way of taking a small, often incomplete view of the world and making it an entire worldview. Let me explain by first reminding you of the parable of the blind men and the elephant. You may remember it. The story, which scholars believe originated in China in the third century A.D., tells of six blind men who grab the elephant at different places on its body and then proceed to describe the elephant. Because each man is blind and can't see the whole, and because each man grabs the elephant at a different place, each comes up with a totally different description. The man who touches the leg says the elephant is like a tree trunk. The man who grabs the tail says it is like a rope. Each one describes accurately what he touches, but he makes a logical error when he attempts to describe the entire elephant based on the small part he has touched.

The nineteenth-century poet John Godfrey Saxe turned this parable into a poem, and it concluded with this verse:

So, oft in theologic wars
    The disputants, I ween [suppose],
Rail on in utter ignorance
    Of what each other mean;
And prate about an Elephant
    Not one of them has seen![2] (emphasis added)

So it has been with the study of philosophy, politics, and theology since the Enlightenment, in particular. Scholars have sought to explain the universe without God as Creator and sovereign King. There are some who say that nature, or the natural world, is all there is. Natural-*ism* is the result. There are others who say that all meaningful statements are either analytic or conclusively verifiable (or at least confirmable) by observation and experiment—which makes them leery of any theological or metaphysical claims. Logical positiv*ism* is the result.

And while the *-ism* list is long—scientism, pluralism, Darwinism, radical skepticism—some of these ideas burn themselves out over time. The truth is that since they are false or incomplete ideas, they cannot permanently sustain themselves. Eventually, even the adherents of false worldviews understand they are false. Indeed, one of the most convincing claims that Christianity and the Judeo-Christian worldview is true is its durability—the fact that despite attacks by virtually all comers, the core truths of Christianity have never been convincingly refuted.

Some of the *-Isms* You Will Encounter

But in the meantime, these *-isms* can do great damage by leading many astray. That is why I'm going to devote much of the rest of this chapter to a brief discussion of some of the more prevalent *-isms* in the American university today, along with some ideas that may help you in rebutting them.

Naturalism

Naturalism is the belief that the natural world is all there is. Some Christian thinkers, including J. Budziszewski, define naturalism as saying that "nothing supernatural is real. If naturalism is true, then there isn't any God."[3] There is an elegant logic to this statement: If only the natural world is real, then anything that is not natural—the supernatural—can't be real.

But that might be dismissing naturalism a bit too lightly, for there are really two (and some would say many more) kinds of naturalism: metaphysical naturalism and methodological naturalism.

Metaphysical naturalism

Metaphysical naturalism is sometimes called "philosophical naturalism" or "ontological naturalism." Ontology is the study of being. Ontology is an attempt to say how we know that something is real. This form of naturalism positively asserts that the metaphysical cannot exist. This view requires a strong atheism—a belief that there is no God.

Overheard in the Student Lounge

In a class on public speaking, I gave a speech against abortion. I worked day and night on my outlines and notes. I pinned my whole arguments against abortion and in support of life on Bible verses. I practiced my speech and did my best to deliver it. At the end, one person simply said, "That's okay, but I don't accept the Bible." I was speechless! I didn't know what to say. The professor had been okay with me delivering a speech that went against the flow. But I didn't argue my point as well as I could have. If you are going to represent Christ and the biblical worldview effectively, make sure that you are fully prepared.

—Holly K., University of Iowa

I'm not going to spend a lot of time on atheism here, because I write more on the existence of God in chapter 6 and because, in reality, few people actually hold an ironclad atheism—not even college professors. As my colleagues Norman Geisler and Frank Turek wrote in *I Don't Have Enough Faith to Be an Atheist*, all worldviews require an element of faith.[4] Geisler and Turek argue that it requires more faith to be an atheist than it does to be a Christian, because in order to positively assert that God does not exist, you must believe that you have a full, complete, and infinite knowledge of the universe. Most people, even those vigorously opposed to the Christian God, will not admit that they have such knowledge. Therefore, it is logically impossible to rule out the chance that God may exist in some form or in some manner that is currently unknown.

That is why less than 2 percent of Americans identify themselves as atheists. Almost everybody believes in something, and even those who don't believe in God know that.

Methodological naturalism

The more rampant form of naturalism on the university campus is methodological naturalism. Methodological naturalism is a belief in process rather than in the end result of the process.

Methodological naturalism is essentially the application of the scientific method to philosophical questions. The scientific method insists that data be based on observable, repeatable events in order for the truth of something to be established. We know that gravity is real, for example, because we can observe it every time we drop a ball. Most college professors who are methodological naturalists would not assert positively that God does not exist but would say that the existence of God has not been proven. Some might even say that the existence of God cannot be proven.

So methodological naturalists don't walk around saying, "I am a methodological naturalist." They are much more likely to say, "I am an agnostic." But it is important to know that methodological naturalism is the -*ism* behind their agnosticism (itself an -*ism*, by the way!).

Because methodological naturalism has much in common with the scientific method with its insistence on observable, repeatable events as a basis for truth, it is no surprise that many in the science departments of most modern universities are full of methodological naturalists. Methodological naturalism's most common expression in biology departments is in the form of Darwinism.

But what I want you to see about methodological naturalism is that its insistence on observable, repeatable events as the basis for truth is its biggest weakness. It ignores the fact that this method is not the exclusive way that we come to our view of truth. We make many conclusions about history, not based on our ability to see or repeat the actions of history, but based on the evidence left behind and the testimony of credible witnesses.

So while I have never met Abraham Lincoln, I am convinced that he existed because of the photographs taken of him, the writings he left behind, and the accounts left by those who were there. This evidence does not "prove" that Abraham Lincoln existed to a mathematical or scientific certainty. But I would suggest to you that even a methodological naturalist would call you crazy if you walked into his class and tried to deny the existence of Abraham Lincoln!

So does understanding the fallacies or incompleteness of methodological naturalism mean that God exists. No. But I do want you to see that methodological naturalism is unsatisfactory as a coherent worldview. The scientific method might help us understand how gravity works, but it doesn't explain why gravity exists in the first place.

Darwinism

The publication of Charles Darwin's *The Origin of Species* in 1859 was a pivotal development in the history of scientific and philosophical thought. Many of the words and phrases that we associate with Darwinism did not even appear in the first edition of the book but were added in the subsequent—and sometimes substantial—revisions that Darwin made on the book as it was reprinted over the course of his lifetime. The word *evolution* and the phrase "survival of the fittest," as examples, did not appear until the fifth edition, published in the early 1870s.

Darwin often made his revisions to counter specific objections to his ideas—objections that began to appear almost immediately.

Relativism

The phrase "everything's relative" falls from the mouths of Christians and non-Christians alike. And in a purely practical sense, there is something to be said for the idea that "everything" is relative. For example, if I asked, "How much is $10?" you could answer in a variety of ways. You could say, "Ten dollars is equal to 10 one-dollar bills." Or you could say, "It is a lot of money to pay for a piece of bubble gum." Or you could say, "It is not a lot of money to pay for an automobile." You might even answer, "It's not a lot of money to Bill Gates, but it is a lot of money to me."

In other words, "It's all relative."

But in the realm of philosophy, *relativism* has a specific meaning. Relativism is the idea that there are no absolute truths. It could be that because of the examples I gave above we have become conditioned to accept the idea of moral or philosophical relativism, but to do so would be to make a grave logical and spiritual error. But before I explain that, let's look at a brief history of relativism.

Relativism became an important part of Western culture with Einstein's theory of relativity, first articulated in the early twentieth century. The beginning of modern times is defined by a convergence of events in the early part of the century that included World War I, the emergence of Einstein's theory, and the wide dissemination of communication and transportation capabilities, which had the impact on the popular imagination of breaking down older conceptions of time and space.[5]

These events and innovations were profound. In the realm of science and technology, many things that had previously been thought to be true were found baseless. Many things that were thought to be impossible, from air travel to the willful annihilation of millions of human beings in war or tyranny, were now demonstrated to be true. Many people began to wonder: "What else that I thought was true might end up being false?"

Of course, many thoughtful people had asked this question through the ages, and the true roots of relativism go back to ancient times. The Sophists of the fifth century B.C., in part as a rebellion to the complex cosmology of Greek gods, originated the phrase, "Man is the measure of all things." I could even argue that relativism began in the Garden of Eden, when the serpent told Eve, "You can be as God."

And that brings us to the grave logical and spiritual error of relativism when it is applied outside the realm of physics. From the Judeo-Christian point of view, the grave spiritual error is easy to define when it comes to the metaphysical and spiritual realms. Relativism is idolatry. God says, "I AM WHO I AM" (Exodus 3:14). He tells us, "I am the LORD your God. . . . You shall have no other gods before me" (Exodus 20:2-3). Relativism retorts, "Says who?" In other words, relativism denies God.

Of course, this grave spiritual error would not matter to a relativist. Why would he care that he has dissed a God he doesn't believe in? But it is important to remember that a relativist must also deny the existence of absolute truth and morality. This is where the relativist falls into the same logical error that snares the atheist. By denying that absolute truth exists, the relativist must make an absolute assertion—"There is no truth"—and that itself violates the assertion. Once again, an effective way to respond to the relativist is with the simple question: "Are you sure?" It's a question the relativist can't answer without hanging himself with his own logic. Some people might assert that there is truth but we can't discover it. They can share the noose with the relativist in that once they assert a truth can't be discovered, they have done just that.

Pluralism

Proponents of pluralism define the term, in its broadest sense, as the acceptance of diversity. But on the university campus it has come to mean that any political or religious ideology must be accepted without criticism. Any objection to any ideology, no matter how extreme, is seen as a threat to pluralism.

It is no surprise, then, that those who wish to promote homosexuality or other behaviors and worldviews that run counter to biblical Christianity will first promote pluralism, diversity, and multiculturalism. Once these values are firmly established, they will use these values—and the policies that institutionalize them—to tear down Christianity.

The University of Chicago started a gay studies project in 1997, and the University of Minnesota is setting up a center for gay, lesbian, bisexual, and transgender studies. Virtually every major secular university in the country has at least one course on homosexual literature, often promoted under the heading of "queer theory," which looks at homosexuality as a legitimate social and literary movement. Some faculty members teach nothing but queer theory classes.

"Gay faculty at colleges and universities across the country are a lot more comfortable asking to teach these courses than they used to be," says Martin Duberman, a distinguished professor of history at the City University of New York and founder of the school's Center for Lesbian and Gay Studies.[6]

A Word from the Faculty

- God embodies truth, and He has told us to love Him with our minds (Matthew 22:37). The beauty and coherence of the biblical worldview stands strong; we do not need to pad the evidence in order to make Christianity sound more convincing.
- When trying to "give a reason for the hope that is in you" (1 Peter 3:15, NKJV), make sure you know how strong your arguments are and aren't. Counterarguments to every worldview exist, including arguments against Christianity. Simply because they exist does not mean, however, that they are compelling arguments.
- A literal translation of Philippians 4:5 is "Let your sweet reasonableness be known to all men; the Lord is near." This reminds me that I don't have to be combative or defensive to be effective.

—*W. Gary Phillips, Th.D., adjunct professor of biblical studies,*
Southern Evangelical Seminary,
pastor, Signal Mountain Bible Church, Tennessee

Utopianism

Utopianism is the idea that humankind can create an ideal world. At the core of utopianism is the concept that man can be as God. Utopianism would have us believe that man is ultimately perfectible. With enough hard work, trial and error, and evolutionary advancement, we will eliminate war, poverty, disease, and selfishness.

The word *utopia* was coined in 1516 by Sir Thomas More, who wrote of the imaginary island of Utopia, where people lived in harmony, free from poverty, tyranny, and war. But More, a devout Catholic who was ultimately martyred for his devotion to his faith, had no illusions that Utopia could be achieved by man. In fact, he exercised a bit of irony and subtlety in coining the word itself. *Utopia* is a combination of two Greek words, and the prefix carries a double entendre. Utopia can mean "good place" or also "no place." In other words, More's Utopia cannot really exist.

Our most insightful modern writers have understood that utopias are impossible, and their works have been not utopian, but *dys*topian. Writers such as George Orwell, in his classic novel *1984*, help us understand that when man attempts to implement his vision of a perfect future, the first step is to erase history, and the final outcome is tyranny and brutality.

You may think that no one actually believes in utopianism, and the concept of utopianism has been so discredited that few people will actually admit that they are utopians. But utopianism is an integral part of the worldview not only on the university campus, but also in the modern political world. Many political liberals are passionate because of their utopian dreams. The belief that massive government social programs will eventually eliminate poverty is a utopian ideal.

To be fair, the impulse to make the world a better place is a noble one, to work hard to do good is not a dishonorable impulse. The problem with utopianism is that *good* and *better* are utterly subjective ideas. *Good* in these cases is defined, not by God or the Bible, but by man. It is no accident of history that the modern university has come to be called the "ivory tower." In *The Iliad,* two kinds of dreams or ghosts emerge from the underworld. "True" dreams emerge from the Gate of Horn. "False" dreams emerge from the Gate of Ivory and "ascend into the upper air." This idea of false dreams living in the ivory tower tells us a great deal about how university academics view the world.

Postmodernism

As we have gone along in this book, we have from time to time referred to "modernism" and "postmodernism." In some ways they are both the simplest and the most difficult concepts to define—in large part because even those who are in general philosophical agreement disagree on the definitions of the terms.

The problem of defining postmodernism has been a problem for some very smart people. One of the smartest of them is the Christian thinker James Sire, who devotes an entire section of his book *The Universe Next Door* to what he calls "The Problem of Definition" when it comes to postmodernism.

But in some ways this problem of definition is the only primary distinguishing characteristic of postmodernism. The cry of the modernist is an assertion: "God (capital G) is dead, and now I am a god (little g)." The cry of the postmodernist is more of a whimper: "God is dead, and I now realize that I'm not much of a god myself. Boy, are we messed up." That may sound flippant and irreverent, but that is the essence of postmodernism. Ihab Hassan, a literature professor who was one of the first to use the word *postmodernism* in the early 1970s, acknowledges this definition problem. He confesses, "I know less about postmodernity than I did thirty years ago. . . . [There is] no consensus . . . on what postmodernism really means." But he says that postmodern culture is characterized by "fragments, hybridity, relativism, play, parody, pastiche, an ironic anti-ideological stance, an ethos bordering on kitsch and camp."[7]

Music sampling in rap music, retro clothing, the "mockumentary" *Borat*—these are all postmodern expressions. They are the postmodern culture's way of acknowledging that we have no current, authentic reality, so we're cobbling things together the best we can. Said more philosophically: God is dead, but I don't feel all that bad.

We Can Be as God—NOT!

You may have discovered that the central idea of all of the *-isms* we have explored in this chapter is that humankind is the center of the universe. It is man's judgments and man's preferences that reign supreme. Or, in the case of postmodernism, the universe has no center, but instead of that being a bad thing, it's a good thing, or at least an okay thing.

Alex on His Soapbox

Some would say, "There is a God, and I am he." Or so they think. Saying so doesn't make it so. Just ask your siblings, your mother, or your best friend. Whether this is a real spiritual belief or a manner of acting—like people owe you the world— it is not realistic. Our heart attitude should be like Christ's: Be ready to serve. One of my favorite Mark Twain quotes is this: "Don't go around saying the world owes you a living. The world owes you nothing. It was here first."[8]

We have talked about the modern manifestations of these ideas, and these modern manifestations have been born in the past few hundred years. Some of them, like relativism, came to prominence in the twentieth century. Darwinism and socialism are nineteenth-century phenomena. Naturalism saw its rise in the eighteenth century as a result of the Enlightenment. Postmodernism is in full flower in this century.

But the truth is that these ideas are not new. As I have mentioned, these *-isms* are just new ways to express one of the oldest ideas in the Bible: Man wants to be his own God. Because I have mentioned this a few times now, and because I want to make a couple of specific points about where we go from here, let's look at a few verses again:

> Now the serpent was more crafty than any of the wild animals
> the LORD God had made. He said to the woman, "Did God
> really say, 'You must not eat from any tree in the garden'?"
>   The woman said to the serpent, "We may eat fruit from
> the trees in the garden, but God did say, 'You must not eat
> fruit from the tree that is in the middle of the garden, and you
> must not touch it, or you will die.' "
>   "You will not surely die," the serpent said to the woman.
> "For God knows that when you eat of it your eyes will be
> opened, and you will be like God, knowing good and evil."
> (Genesis 3:1-5)

The serpent's strategy is indeed crafty. Even the serpent knew that if God said it, then it was settled. So first he questions whether God really said what He said. His only hope was to get the woman to question whether God really said what she remembered. When the woman confirmed that God had indeed said to stay away from that tree, the serpent uses his secret weapon: He tells the woman that she can be like God.

That insight is also our secret weapon in evaluating the -*isms* of the world. They are all attempts to replace God with one or many lesser gods—including our very selves.

Resisting the -*isms* of the Academy

So what are our ultimate defenses against the "-*isms* of the academy"? I want, once again, to say that there are no easy answers to most of the tough questions and ideas we are discussing. In fact, one of the problems with today's culture, which in fact led to some of the -*isms* we're struggling with, is that we too often want easy answers. But here are a few suggestions that will help you deal with some of those philosophical challenges.

Don't be too proud to admit your ignorance

When you are in a discussion with someone who has a question you can't answer, don't be too proud to admit that you don't know the answer. By admitting you don't know an answer, you'll impress the other person with your intellectual honesty. That may have more of an effect on him or her than any brilliant answer you could produce. Remember, just because you don't know the answer doesn't mean there is not an answer. I don't know how my microwave works, but it works. Say to the other person, "That's a great question, and I don't know the answer, but I am sure going to try to find out."

Have spiritual and intellectual mentors

I have been blessed to have in my life a number of go-to guys who can help me when I get myself in situations like the one in the paragraph above. In the field of philosophy and apologetics, that person was Norman Geisler. Dr. Geisler was my professor and mentor when I was in graduate school at Liberty University, and when I took over from him as president of Southern Evangelical Seminary, I made a weekly discipleship session with him one of the conditions of my employment.

In the past few years, I have been blessed with the opportunity to write hundreds of articles and several books—one of which you're holding in your hand. As a preacher and seminary professor, I'm pretty good with words, but writing is a discipline different from preaching, and I've needed coaching in it. Tom Neven, who oversees publications at Focus on the Family, has been one of my literary mentors.

I share this with you to make this point: You can't have an answer for everything the moment you step onto a college campus. After all, if you did, you wouldn't need to go to college in the first place.

Don't argue with your professor

You are likely to have a professor who is committed to one or more of the *-isms* we have discussed in this chapter. Arguing with your professor is about the worst thing you can do. For one thing, even if you are right and he is wrong, it is likely that many years in the classroom has made him a more skillful debater than you are. Second, it is important to remember that the purpose of engaging nonbelievers in these sorts of discussions is not to win arguments, but to win them to Christ. Too often, we Christians forget that the person we are arguing with is not the enemy. He or she is in bondage to the enemy. Sometimes I think that Satan must get a big kick out of the way we Christians pummel non-Christians with our arguments. Speak the truth? Absolutely! But do so with love. Again, our goal is to win their hearts, not humiliate them in an argument.

One of the most effective ways to destroy falsehood is to ask probing questions. If something is true, it can stand the scrutiny of tough questions. If a position or philosophy is not true, it will unravel.

I am not a huge fan of the *Dr. Phil* television program, but he does something that I think is shrewd. He asks what I call "process questions." For example, when someone on his program says something false or outrageous, or does something destructive, Dr. Phil often asks this question: "How's that workin' for ya?" Now, Dr. Phil already knows that the belief or behavior in question is false and destructive, but he also knows that simply telling the person that it is false and destructive is not likely to do much good. The person needs to come to that conclusion on his or her own.

By the Book

Do not conform any longer to the pattern of this world, but be transformed by the renewing of your mind. Then you will be able to test and approve what God's will is—his good, pleasing and perfect will.

—Romans 12:2

■ ■ ■

It is not enough to have a good mind. The main thing is to use it well.

—René Descartes, French philosopher,
mathematician, and scientist (1596–1650)[9]

■ ■ ■

The philosopher ought never to try to avoid the duty of making up his mind.

—Mortimer Adler, American
philosopher (1902–2001)[10]

In the area of philosophy and theology, I have two favorite process questions I love to ask people who are pursuing false and destructive *-isms.*

- *That's an interesting philosophy. What's happened to the people who have followed it?*
- *When those ideas became popular, what were the results?*

Another set of questions to ask is what I call "consequence questions." All ideas have consequences.

- *Can you say more about that?* Most of the *-isms* we have discussed sound good at first blush but don't hold up under even the most basic scrutiny. It usually doesn't take long for inconsistencies to show themselves.
- *What would happen if everyone did that?* If something is good and true for one person, it should be good and true for all.
- *How can we know that this is true?* A relativist has a tough time answering this question, thereby casting doubt on his entire worldview.
- *Has anyone tried that, and, if so, what happened?* Bad ideas come to disastrous ends. Cultures that have pursued the *-isms* of this chapter have all come to ruin.

There are many more consequence questions, but most of the best ones begin with the word *why.* Christianity answers the great "why" questions of life, and no other worldview can.

EVERYTEEN David

By the end of October, David had found a niche with some guys in his accounting classes. He began hanging out with them in their dorm lounges and went to concerts with them on the weekends. His questions about God were put on the back burner—that is, until he caught some footage of the Dalai Lama on YouTube and began reading Thoreau in English literature class. He liked the Dalai Lama's humanitarian efforts and liked the notion of transcendentalism, that one achieves insight via personal intuition rather than religious doctrine. *There is a God,* he decided. *But who can really say that the ancient texts of the Bible are the only truths?*

Chapter 6

Logic, Philosophy, and God

For the foolishness of God is wiser than
man's wisdom, and the weakness of God
is **strong**er than man's strength.

—*I Corinthians 1:25*

I often speak on college campuses on the reality of God and the existence of truth. One day after one of my presentations, a professor said there was no such thing as truth. It was during a question-and-answer session, but the truth is that this professor had no questions. He wanted to rant: God isn't real. Truth does not exist. Religion is a crutch. It's all a fake and a fraud.

When the professor was finished, I let a pregnant pause fill the auditorium and then asked this simple question:

"Are you sure?"

That simple question exposes the logical fallacies and contradictions of his position. Think about it. If he is *sure* that there is no such thing as truth, doesn't that idea become the new truth? If he is consistent to his own statement, he can't say that he is *sure* there is no such thing as truth. Such confidence would contradict his own assertion that there is no truth!

And that is really my point. Truth exists. This is an unavoidable conclusion. Even if you say, "Truth does not exist," that statement itself claims to be truth.

So the real question is not "Does truth exist?" Rather, the real question is this: What is truth, and how can we know it?

The Death of Reason

This professor isn't alone in his thinking. Every day on American campuses Christians are being opposed by professors and administrators who believe one of the *-isms* we discussed in the last chapter: multiculturalism (or diversity). In the current culture, multiculturalism is a higher pursuit than the quest for truth.

What is ironic here is that colleges have long been a place where the pursuit of truth has been valued. When Harvard College was founded, it adopted as its motto the Latin word *veritas*, or "truth." But what is ironic is also potentially tragic, as what is at stake on campuses isn't just the fair representation of Christianity; it's the question of whether or not truth exists at all.

In my book *The Ten Most Common Objections to Christianity*, I recounted a story that happened on a college campus in my native North Carolina.

Several years ago, a prominent North Carolina–based university attempted to prohibit a chapter of Campus Crusade for Christ from becoming chartered at the school. Some students apparently objected to having the respected ministry at this particular college, and opposition from the faculty came even from the school's president and campus minister.

Despite this college's Baptist origins, despite a wide variety of other groups welcoming this chapter, and despite a significant portion of the students favoring the ministry's presence at the school, Campus Crusade was denied access because of its distinctively evangelical beliefs. A representative from the school was asked to elaborate on her campus's policy on tolerance and diversity. She responded by saying that if a certain ideology was offensive to even *one person,* that viewpoint or attitude should not be allowed on campus. She failed to see that her cherished political correctness could not pass even its own test, for many students found *it* to be offensive.

Aristotle, often called the "father of logic," taught that there are certain things that all rational people can grasp intuitively. Indeed, God hardwired us to instinctively recognize basic truths, things the writers of the Declaration of Independence called "self-evident." So if you sensed a red flag rising in the back of your mind as you read through both this woman's comments and those of the professor mentioned earlier, it's because God gave you the ability to recognize a contradiction.

As Christians, we should cultivate this ability to spot the contradictions that pervade much of the conventional wisdom of our day. Since it seems no one else will, we must be the ones to point out that the emperor is actually naked and that in the act of arguing *against* truth, skeptics are inherently assuming that something can be true— namely, their statements against truth. Whether it's on college campuses, at work, or in church, we must contend that truth not only *exists,* but that it is also *knowable.* Both are undeniable propositions. Beyond that, college leaders like those at the formerly Baptist school in North Carolina need to be reminded that once you define what is or is not "acceptable" diversity, you have ceased to be diverse.

The truth-obstructing fallacies that underlie popular notions of tolerance must be exposed. Of course, explaining the gospel message and leading a person to trust Christ are two different matters. But at least by helping people see the undeniable existence *of* truth, we can help point the way to a relationship with the One who *is* truth.

EVERYTEEN Joel

After researching the validity of the Bible's historicity, Joel came to the conclusion that it could be trusted. And the evidence for believing wasn't flimsy, either. Talk about obsessive-compulsive! The Old Testament manuscripts have been meticulously copied and preserved for over a thousand years. He found that the New Testament has even more validity, especially in archaeology. (See Appendix I, question 6.) Additionally he liked the fact that the Bible had at least 40 authors, was written over a period of 1,500 years, and yet has a harmonious and unified message. Compared to the Book of Mormon, which had only one writer and virtually no corroborating archaeological evidence, the Bible was a much more trustworthy document.

But did its being historically accurate make it true?

Life Without God

Discussing the existence of truth with someone can be an especially difficult task if that person is an atheist, since atheists often give off an air of intellectual superiority. But as smart and innovative as they can seem at times, the truth is, atheism has been around since the beginning of human history. Humans have always tried, starting in the Garden of Eden, to push God out of the picture and establish life apart from Him. In all our arrogance, we've spent thousands of years trying to rationalize the Creator out of creation's existence.

Every atheist carries with him a spiritual and emotional laundry bag full of reasons not to believe in God. Tragically, few of those reasons deal solely with God Himself. Instead, they're based on the *per-*

ception of God, which is usually determined by extraneous factors. Many atheists have been spiritually abused. After one too many hypocritical Christians did them wrong or judged before loving, they

Overheard in the Student Lounge

My professor in a freshman history class often made the comment that the God of Islam and the God of Christianity are one and the same. This freshman history class also included days of lectures explaining the beliefs of Buddhism and Islam, with various pictures, slides, and notes.

Someone asked, "Are we going to study the great Reformation that swept through Europe 400 years ago?" The professor rolled his eyes like the question was stupid, and asked, "Do we have any Protestants in here?"

No one spoke. It is tough to express how I felt, but I wanted to raise my hand and say something in defense of how Christianity had influenced the world. But I kept silent. I didn't know what to say.

Although most of our professors are God-haters, we do have a growing Christian presence among the students on our campus. Students from Christian organizations are hard at work and constantly pray for our campus to see revival.

I think that all hope is not gone. The apologetics I have learned have given me a lot to share. And this information really does get people's attention. Even some of the professors have admitted that they didn't know there were so many historical facts that back up Christianity.

—*Andrew M., Connecticut*

decided if following God looks like *that*, why be a part of it? Others have fatherhood issues based on being raised by a deadbeat or abusive dad. Others may have once believed in God, but when He failed to answer a prayer they became angry and chose to say He didn't exist rather than wrestle through the tough issue of unanswered prayer. Whatever the issue, it's common for atheists to project those problems onto their concept of God (or lack thereof), which simply reinforces their belief that He doesn't exist.

A Word from the Faculty

While attending a major university in the South, my faith was shaken by an anthropology course. The professor lined up half a dozen skulls across the front of his desk. He explained that the primitive-looking skull on the left belonged to a subhuman species. He worked his way across the desk to the right, using each skull to explain how humans had evolved from primates.

The professor told my class, "People used to believe that God created life, but now we know that no supernatural force or deity had anything to do with it." Now skip from anthropology to psychology class, where the professor said, "We know that God had nothing to do with creation. Face it: Evolution and atheism have the better arguments."

Though I had been an active Christian, in my heart I stopped believing in God. I was afraid to tell my Christian friends I was an atheist. I wanted to believe in God and trust the Bible. I wanted to once again have Jesus as my Savior, but I assumed that I could never again believe. The "intellectual" climate of my university had convinced me that humans had evolved apart from

Before we move on, let's clear something up. It's important to understand that unbelief in God can take one of two forms: atheism or agnosticism. Atheism says there is no God, while agnosticism believes you can't know for sure whether there's a God. An atheist completely rules God out. An agnostic, perhaps intent on being more open-minded, rules out only the possibility of certain knowledge of God.

Both are wrong. But an honest agnostic has more going for him or her in the logic category than an avowed atheist. Because to be a

God. Christianity was a mythological relic from simpler times, still held today only by simple people. No "thinking" person would question science, because science is the only true way to know anything for sure.

But a fellow student gave me hope. He gave me a cassette tape of a creationist debating an evolutionist. The evolutionist stammered and stuttered, while the creationist gave clear, compelling arguments for his position.

My Christian faith was eventually fully restored as I read Christian apologetics books. Today, I teach in a Christian high school. I tell my students they need to know how to defend their faith.

The teens say, "Sure, sure, we hear you. I would never waver in my faith." But I am living proof that the pressure of the campus can make a strong, dedicated Christian have doubts—and possibly abandon the faith. For a dark period, I lived as a "regenerated atheist." Fortunately, God led me back to Himself.

—*Brian Henson, M.A. in biblical archaeology from Wheaton College*

true atheist requires not only a rejection of God, but an active accept-ance of many beliefs that, I would argue, are much more difficult to believe than God!

But more about that later. For now, let's examine some of the fatal flaws found in both atheism and agnosticism.

Atheism and Agnosticism

Most atheists fail to acknowledge something foundational about their belief: Atheism requires omniscience, which is complete knowledge of everything.

If you don't believe that, then consider this. The only way anyone can assert that there is no God would be to presume that he knew everything about *everything*. Otherwise, there would always be a pos-sibility that God, in fact, existed, but He is just outside knowledge or our ability to know.

Obviously, it's not possible for one man to know everything about the universe. Yet atheists say that nothing exists outside of the mate-rial world, placing them in a godlike position. I'm sure that Colum-bus, Magellan, Cortez, or any other explorer would chuckle at the arrogance of this notion. Even people during their time who thought the world was flat still believed there was something else out there.

In reality, this intellectual position is the height of arrogance. But atheists tend to disguise this arrogance with intellectualism. In his best-selling book *Cosmos,* renowned evolutionist/atheist Carl Sagan proclaimed, "The Cosmos is all that is or ever was or ever will be."[1] Sagan believed humans should move beyond the age-old belief that life had been the special creation of a personal God. He spoke for mul-titudes of evolutionists in asserting that humans were simply an evo-lutionary accident, "a mote of dust in the morning sky." Such admissions, Sagan wrote, were "not, I think, irreverent, although they may trouble whatever gods may be."[2] However, Sagan didn't mean the God of the Bible when he said this. Rather, he means what he believes to be man-made gods and superstitions.

But in following Sagan's line of thought that the "Cosmos is all that is or ever was or ever will be," consider what would be required for someone to accept with certainty that this is true. Again, to rule out even the possibility that a God exists and is a creator of the Cosmos would require omniscience on the part of the person making that claim. Often, the language of atheists communicates a kind of false humility, as we could see in the quote by Sagan, when he described huhumankind as a "mote of dust in the morning sky." But this artful and falsely humble language masks the reality of this thought process: an attempt to make themselves into gods. That, in a way, is the ultimate irony: Atheists, in their denial of God, cannot help but replace the truly omniscient God with a poor imitation—themselves!

Yet still atheists will argue that faith in the God of Scripture is simply naive, a more primitive system of thought, if you will. Their logical blind spots remind me of a line from the Will Smith movie *I, Robot*. The actor plays a cynical cop in the future who seems to be

Alex on His Soapbox

Don't be afraid to ask questions. Don't feel as if you have to know it all the first day of school. Whatever you do, do not be afraid to ask questions of everybody—where is the business office, what is the deadline to drop a class, is there a shortcut between the biology building and the library, where is a good church, do any churches have free meals on Wednesdays? You won't look foolish asking questions; you will look foolish if you don't.

the only person on earth open to the slight possibility that a robot could develop beyond the scope of its creator's design. Teamed up with a theory-driven, numbers-based scientist, Smith becomes exasperated by the woman's refusal to accept anything outside her system of belief. He yells at her, "You are [the] dumbest, smart person . . . I have ever met in my life!"[3]

The Built-in Contradiction

Agnostics aren't that different from atheists in that their beliefs are built on contradictory assertions. As we've just discussed, an atheist can't truthfully say that God doesn't exist since he doesn't have all knowledge. An agnostic, on the other hand, claims that you can't know for sure whether God exists or not.

But think about it: By claiming that you can't really know anything for sure about God, you've done the very thing! In making such a statement, you therefore know *something*—namely, that He can't be known. In other words, it's a contradiction to say, "One thing I know about God: You can't know anything about Him." Yet that's exactly what an agnostic says. Talk about being double-minded!

I've spoken on many college campuses throughout the years. And without a doubt, when presenting this side of the argument against agnosticism, I've had a couple of fervent students fire back, "Okay, I'll buy into the notion that God exists. But that's all we can know about Him. It's impossible to know anything specific beyond that."

My usual response goes something like this: "Wait a minute! Listen to what you're saying, because in your own words you've already established a couple of things. One, He exists; and two—you know something about Him. In saying that you can't know anything about God, you're claiming to know at least *one thing* about Him."

Not Up for Debate

It's interesting that the Bible never addresses the question of whether God exists. From Genesis through the last letters of Revelation, the existence of God is a given.

"Well, sure—*that's* a given," some would argue. "It's the Bible. It wouldn't argue against this since it's the foundational document for those who believe God exists."

That's true. But those same believers also understand that God is big enough to handle any question. He's fully capable of dealing with the most extreme doubters who claim He's nothing more than a human-concocted fairy tale.

So what does Scripture have to say about those doubters, the atheists and agnostics who claim God doesn't exist and can't be known? "The fool says in his heart, 'There is no God'" (Psalm 14:1). Could it be any clearer? The Bible doesn't even address the atheist's flawed ideas except to call them foolish!

God's existence is both undeniable and necessary—and not just for Christians. In the following sections, we'll deal with some of the proofs that demonstrate this truth. No, they're not passionate, emotional appeals to believe in this unseen God. They're simply logic-based reasons that appeal to our common sense. And strangely enough, God created us with common sense. Though we may be often fooled by lies and delusions, remember that we're hardwired with the ability to recognize contradictions. We're prone to spot things that just don't make sense.

Remember the story of *Alice in Wonderland*? One reason people love the tale is because of its nonsensical nature. It's full of contradictions that border on the absurd—yet that's the very reason we enjoy this fanciful whirlwind adventure. We chuckle when the Mad Hatter makes such statements as, "Have some tea, there isn't any," because we know this makes absolutely no sense. Throughout the book, author Lewis Carroll (who was an ordained minister) is simply playing with the English language—and with our sense of reasoning—to make a point. He turns things upside down and backward to show the foolishness of illogical reasoning. No matter how passionate or "intellectual" we get in our arguments, some things just don't add up.

It's no different than what our culture calls the fundamental question of spirituality: Does God exist? As you'll see through the following proofs, that's as off base as asking if water is a liquid, or if the sky is blue, or if gravity is real.

I. Every effect has a cause

We all learned in science class that every effect has a cause. An uncaused effect is an impossibility. Stated another way, you can't have an outcome or consequence without having something to cause that result. Likewise, it's hard to imagine the universe not having a source behind it. Even atheists believe the universe itself is a massive effect. Evolutionists believe its cause came from a Big Bang billions of years ago. Christians credit the source as almighty God. Either way, both science and Scripture acknowledge that the universe had a beginning. Science has proven it through such means as the Hubble telescope; Scripture simply states it as understood truth.

So the question up for debate isn't whether the universe has an origin; it's who—or what—prompted that beginning. Imagine you're sitting in your living room enjoying a peaceful afternoon while reading the paper. Suddenly, a baseball flies into the room, shattering your window. Obviously, your first question wouldn't be, "How did that get here?" It would be, in a highly bothered tone, "Who did this?!" The baseball didn't just smash through your window on its own.

Some agent acted upon it, causing a "disturbance in the force" that ruined your perfectly good afternoon.

The point is, the universe couldn't have just arrived with no force behind it. And unlike the remote possibility that a pitching machine in your neighbor's yard turned itself on and spat a baseball into your living room—which is still a cause—it's virtually impossible that a universe was just spat out by an inanimate force. It took a Person, a Someone. We Christians believe that to be the God of the Bible, the Great Cause.

2. Every creation has a creator

In the same way, it's impossible for something to be created void of a creator. Something that's made has to have a maker. Both creationists and evolutionists agree that life didn't just suddenly appear; it was made possible by something (a Big Bang) or someone (God). The universe is a creation, and the earth's life cycle clearly proves that.

Going one step further, however, Genesis states that God is responsible for creation. The first two chapters serve as "the account of the heavens and the earth when they were created. When the LORD God made the earth and the heavens" (2:4). Obviously, some people think of the biblical creation account as a fairy tale that lacks substance. Yet if all creation serves as proof of a Creator, who—or what—else could be responsible?

3. Every design has a designer

Watch a sunset. Stare at the waves of the ocean. Examine a leaf or a flower. Hold a newborn baby. Our eyes don't have to travel far to find proof that the earth was intricately designed. The world around us is bursting with wonderful, breathtaking design. And following suit with the previous two proofs, this implies that behind the design is an Ultimate Designer.

But there's more. The complexity of the earth's designs—from the mesmerizing patterns of nature to the awesome uniqueness of a DNA strand—tells us that this designer is *intelligent*. The patterns of life are obviously not mindless happenstance.

Think of it another way: Cars go through a systemized process in their formation. They don't just build themselves from iron and elements found in soil; they're formed and fashioned in automobile factories. Likewise, concertos are birthed through composers, paintings come from painters, and inventions come from inventors. Each product is uniquely created by the hands of a person. If we acknowledge that this world consists of incredible and intricate designs, how can we not point to the hands of a designer?

4. Communication requires a communicator

Scientists agree that the universe around us is constantly communicating with us. When we hear this, most of us imagine some half-crazed researcher spending decades listening to static noise from outer space, waiting for some abnormal yet distinct pattern or variance. The 1997 movie *Contact*, based on Carl Sagan's 1985 book of the same name, gave us a glamorized version of the search for extraterrestrial intelligence. In it, Dr. Ellie Arroway (played by Jodie Foster) is monitoring radio waves and signals from outer space, listening for some sort of ordered, encrypted sequence in the midst of static. She and other scientists eventually decipher a pattern of prime numbers, a signal that is, as they describe it, "not a natural phenomenon." As a result, they surmise that a complex, ordered pattern can only come from an extraterrestrial source—an intelligent source.[4]

Yet such communication can be found in our everyday existence. Consider the fact that the blueprint for who we are is intricately coded within the DNA molecules of our bodies. In other words, the DNA contained in every cell within your body contains information. It's filled with "instructions"—complex, coded information. Obviously, information can't be communicated unless there's a communicator—and in this case, an *intelligent* communicator—delivering the information.

5. Every law has a lawgiver

If you've ever studied sociology, you know that there are some things that people everywhere intuitively recognize, things that are universal and pervade all cultures. One of them is smiling, and another is the existence of moral law. No matter where you go in this world, people inherently recognize the difference between right and wrong. We are born with a conscience that gives us such a filter. Obviously, we don't always *do* what's right—but we *know* what's right.

Imagine traveling to 10 separate islands out in the ocean. On the first island, you discover an unspoken list of do's and don'ts. Even without an official government to rule over them and establish laws, you've noticed that the locals have established their own code of ethics that prohibits such things as murder, theft, adultery, molestation . . . it goes on. As long as everyone abides by these rules, everyone's happy.

When you move on to Island No. 2, you're amazed to find virtually the same moral code, despite the fact that none of these people have ever had any interaction with those on the previous island you visited. Again, certain boundaries have been naturally established.

Coincidentally, the third island you visit has virtually the same laws as Islands No. 1 and No. 2, even though these people again have been completely independent and secluded from the other two. This pattern continues for all 10 islands. And though it's amazing to think of the similarities, it raises several valid thoughts: If the people on all 10 of these islands have never had any interaction with each other, yet all 10 have similar moral codes, wouldn't it be within reason to assume there's a natural inclination aiding the establishment of these laws? Since those on all 10 islands have virtually the same idea of what is right and wrong, isn't it logical to presume this idea came from a third party?

Don't believe it? Think the scenario is a little too theoretical and idealistic?

Believe me, it's not that far-fetched. In C. S. Lewis's *The Abolition of Man*, the author documents cultures throughout all history, presenting some of the common threads that bind every civilization. Among these commonalities are the notions that you shouldn't murder, steal,

By the Book

Reading about nature is fine, but if a person walks in the woods and listens carefully, he can learn more than what is in books, for they speak with the voice of God.

—George Washington Carver, former slave, horticulturist, and inventor of peanut butter (1864–1943)[5]

■ ■ ■

By wisdom the LORD laid the earth's foundations,
by understanding he set the heavens in place;
by his knowledge the deeps were divided,
and the clouds let drop the dew.

—Proverbs 3:19-20

■ ■ ■

In a time of universal deceit, telling the truth becomes a revolutionary act.

—George Orwell, British journalist and author of Animal Farm and 1984 (1903–1950)[6]

sleep with your neighbor's spouse, etc. On the flip side, all cultures esteemed telling the truth, being kind, acting selflessly, etc. In every case, from the Phoenicians to the Egyptians to the Greeks to the Romans to twentieth-century civilization, humans shared a vehement reaction against injustice: theft, rape, murder, pillaging, etc. Meanwhile, they all innately affirmed heroism, altruism, self-denial, etc.

Lewis's study (and others by Christian apologists and sociologists) proved that different people groups and cultures, though having no contact with each other, nevertheless had similar moral codes and ethical structures by which they lived. That's not to say that humans always *do* what is morally right; Lewis and others assert that all cultures intuitively *know* what is right.[7]

Since human knowledge of moral law appears to be ubiquitous, and since different cultures all seem to know moral truth—whether civilized or primitive, urban or rural—the source of moral knowledge must be absolute, rather than subjective. In other words, morality isn't just social mores (a "cultural accident") but is intrinsic and from some outside source (for example, God). There must be an outside lawgiver!

If, then, we've established that we all know the law but don't always live it out to perfection, then that equates to breaking the law. And if we're honest, we must admit that in breaking the law, we've offended the lawgiver. The moral code, then, doesn't just point us to the lawgiver; it also reveals our need for forgiveness and a Savior!

There Must Be Something More

Upon hearing the name Friedrich Nietzsche most educated people immediately think of a single phrase: "God is dead."[8] The outspoken atheist, who once called himself the Antichrist and labeled his brand of thought "philosophizing with a hammer," coined the famous declaration as part of his adamant denial of God's existence. For much of his life, Nietzsche argued that there is no God, no afterlife, and that existence amounts to nothing more than life in this world. But prior to his death, Nietzsche drifted toward insanity and longed for permanence beyond this life. Arguing for what he called "eternal return," he attempted to retain a belief in naturalism and yet also hoped for a world continually being reformed and reborn.

Nearing his death, Nietzsche said, "The eternal hourglass of existence is turned over and over, and you with it, a grain of sand."[9] In his final years, it seemed this tenacious and influential atheist could not come to grips with his own belief that his existence—and personhood —would one day be snuffed out. Even atheists long for what scholars call *transcendence*, something beyond this natural, mortal world.

It's Time to Get Personal

After briefly delving into these five proofs (and obviously, there are more), let me say something that may rock your boat a little: Don't get hung up on any of these as your proof that God exists. Because essentially, these can get us only so far in knowing the "who" behind the "what." These evidences simply lead us to a fuzzy, nebulous supreme being responsible for all of life. In fact, we could have the god of Star Wars—the god of some mysterious "force"—based on what we've discussed so far. (See Appendix I, question 19 for a discussion on "intelligent design.")

Fortunately, there's more. We're not left hanging by an unknown God. Quite the opposite, in fact. If there's one thing we can be sure of, as revealed through creation, history, Jesus Christ, and the Bible, it's that God is personal.

"But I'm still not sure I believe in Jesus or the Bible," you say. That's fine. We'll get there. For now, let's review some things we've already established to arrive at a new and fundamental point.

We concluded that both science and Scripture agree that the universe has a beginning. Was this beginning caused or uncaused? We know that an uncaused effect is impossible; it doesn't exist. Clocks don't wind themselves, baseballs don't throw themselves. So the universe was intentionally caused. If that's the case, we can assume this "Causer" must be personal, since He created personal beings.

How so? Well, simply put, if God isn't personal, then He's less developed than we are. God must *at least* be personal because He created humans to be personal. You and I have a will; we have emotion, personality, volition, ambition. If God isn't a personal God, then He's not as sophisticated as we are, and we (the effect) have eclipsed Him (the Cause). That's not rational. And that also means it's safe to say that because God is in fact the Causer/Creator/Intelligent Designer/Communicator/Lawgiver who is above the effect/creation/design/communication/law, then He is indeed personal.

Okay, Now That We're on a Friendly Basis . . .

What does God's being personal have to do with the price of eggs in China? Remember, the atheist says God doesn't exist. We've already proven the flawed rationale behind that one. Meanwhile, the agnostic says that God may indeed exist but that He can't be known. We've talked about how that's a contradiction; but now that we know God is a personal being, there's more to add. And here's where it gets good.

Not only does God reveal Himself as personal, He invites us to know all about the rest of Him. God is a *revelatory* God. How do we know He's really out there, that He really wants to know us and isn't just tricking us into being mindless robots that say and do whatever He wants? Simply put, because He's already proven Himself. He's shown us and He still is revealing Himself to the world.

How is He doing this? There are four significant ways He shows Himself. In a general way, He proves Himself through the following:

- **Creation**: the universe itself isn't just proof of His existence; it's a snapshot photo of who He is.
- **Conscience**: the basic moral code that's innate in all of us shows us God's standards, which reveal His character.

God has also proven Himself through more specific means:

- **Scripture**: virtually every page of the Bible paints an up-close and personal portrait of God.
- **Savior**: Jesus Christ came as God in flesh to show us firsthand who God is.

Don't worry if you're not sold on these yet, specifically the Bible and Jesus parts. We'll address those later in the book. For now, my point is simply to show you that God doesn't have to be viewed as some out-there, far-off supreme being who can't be described. He is personal, which means there's more of Him that we can know, more about Him that we can discover. Not only can He be searched, He *wants* to be searched (and found)—specifically by you!

EVERYTEEN Joel

Now that Joel was convinced the Bible is an accurate historical document and can be trusted on facts such as the resurrection, he began reading it with much more interest. He joined a Bible study on campus with a friend he had made through his InterVarsity Christian Fellowship connections. And, he had plenty of answers—and more questions—for his roommate, Marshal.

When he was confronted by new ideas in his classes, he took those ideas and compared them to the Scriptures. At times he needed help in figuring everything out, but he knew whom to ask for help. He also knew that real Truth could stand up to the testing.

Chapter 7

Attacks on Biblical Morality

The LORD spoke to me with
his **strong** hand upon me, warning me
not to follow the way of this people.

—*Isaiah 8:11*

Y ou may have heard your parents and youth-group leaders complaining about the "culture war." But all you have to do is scan your browser's home page or pick up the newspaper and you can read articles about abortion, gambling, pornography, same-sex marriage, homosexual rights, and all the other skirmishes in the so-called culture war.

For college students, the mind-numbing constancy of the rhetoric coming from both sides makes it hard to get and stay excited about these issues.

But taking a closer look at the life of our friend EVERYTEEN Cameron brings the culture war a bit closer to home.

EVERYTEEN Cameron

Cameron longed for the validation of his intellect by his peers, his teachers, and his parents, especially his father. But when Cameron went off to college and came out from under the direct influence of his father's judging eye, things changed for him. He had freedom to choose his own paths. His brilliance attracted the attention of a T.A., an openly gay grad student named Nolan. At first Cameron was uncomfortable talking to Nolan; after all, he was president of the gay activist club on campus. Later, as he gained respect for Nolan, Cameron decided to keep quiet about Christianity so that their differences wouldn't spark an argument. And, in his social psychology class, homosexuality was presented as a healthy expression of human love.

Cameron went to the campus-sponsored Internet site to become more informed about the gay lifestyle and Nolan's club. It didn't seem so bad. That "choice" wasn't an option for Cameron, but he thought, *Homosexuality doesn't really harm anyone, right? It's not as if Nolan is a murderer or something. Besides, he can't help his homosexual orientation. He was born that way; at least that's what the scientists say.*

Cameron couldn't imagine Nolan being one of those out-of-control gays who threw condoms at churches or went to gay bars looking for a dozen sex partners in one night. Soon the friendship with Nolan was the most significant one that Cameron had on campus; looking back at his former attitude toward homosexuals, Cameron felt ashamed and ignorant that he once would have said he hated gays.

The College Campus as Battleground

The college campus has always been a place where new and radical ideas are discussed. In one sense, this is a good thing. College should be a time of intellectual exploration and adventure.

But the university should also be a place where wisdom, not propaganda, reigns supreme. Historically, the university was the place where the best ideas and the best art were taught. New ideas were entertained, but they were subjected to rigorous scrutiny and logic. Harvard, our nation's first college, has had a one-word motto for its entire history: *veritas*, which means truth. As the great eighteenth-century poet John Keats put it, the proper pursuits of man are "Beauty is truth, truth beauty,—that is all / Ye know on earth, and all ye need to know."[1]

But that has changed. Today, many if not most of the faculty at Harvard would not profess to believe in an objective truth. In chapter 5's discussion of *-isms,* we spent some time on pluralism. In American universities, pluralism often shows itself as multiculturalism, which is the idea that all cultures and the ideas of these cultures are equal and equally good. Multiculturalism, in its extreme forms, would not allow any differentiation between the best art of the Renaissance and the paintings of cave dwellers.

Don't get me wrong; I think the paintings of cave dwellers are fascinating and should be preserved for their historical significance. But to declare all expressions equally good is both illogical and dangerous. In its modern expression, multiculturalism means that ideas that are demonstrably false, logically questionable, or morally repulsive cannot be expelled from our lives. Queer theory, pedophilia, pornography— all of these and many more have their advocates at the modern university. And when there is any concerted attempt to confront these destructive views, their advocates hide behind the twin towers of multiculturalism and academic freedom.

James Davison Hunter wrote the classic book on the subject, *Culture Wars: The Struggle to Define America.* In it, he focuses on the fight at Stanford University to abolish the Western civilization course, which had previously been a requirement for all students. It's important to note that Western culture means, in large part, the Judeo-Christian culture. A proposal to drop the Western civ course in favor of one called "Culture, Ideas, and Values" was adopted, and, according to Hunter, "still other new course requirements for undergraduates emphasizing racial, ethnic, sexual, and gender-based diversity were established."[2]

And this is not happening just at elite schools such as Stanford. Hunter goes on:

> The situation at Stanford is just the most publicized case of a debate that has been repeated in different ways at most colleges across the country—Columbia, Chicago, Brown, Pennsylvania, Michigan, Minnesota, and Indiana, among others. At the University of Wisconsin, students are required to take ethnic studies courses but are not required to study Western civilization or even American history. Similar measures have been enacted at Dartmouth, Mount Holyoke, and the University of California at Berkeley.[3]

Never far beneath the surface of these debates is a discussion of moral behavior and either an implicit or explicit attack on biblical morality.

Culture War Issues

Given that, let's look at a few of the more common culture-war issues from a biblical perspective.

Abortion

On average, more than a million abortions have occurred every year in America since the landmark Supreme Court decision Roe v. Wade made abortion legal in 1973. That means more than 35 million babies have been aborted in the Roe era. In recent years, even those who

A Word from the Faculty

Over the past 20 years, I've seen an increase in multiculturalism at the college level. One English instructor I knew forced her class to spell woman as womyn. Students flunked if they used *man* within that word.

If you are faced with a similar problem, talk with your professor about reasonable alternatives such as using the dictionary as your spelling reference. If your professor will not accommodate, document the meeting—time, date, location, and outcome. Then make an appointment with the department chair. If that doesn't work, visit your college's dean and work your way up. Meanwhile, go to class and do all other work, all the while documenting what is happening. Make sure you bring a copy of your documentation (never bring the originals) when meeting with someone.

Of course, if you take an anthropology class, realize that evolution will be taught. You should not mark "false" on all your essay questions as one student I know did. Instead, write the "academic" answer (to show yourself responsible) and then write your answer.

To be a true witness, though, you must go above and beyond the quick-let's-get-it-done mentality of most students. Learn the material, remain strong in your beliefs, and develop a relationship with your professors. If you want to be heard in academia, respond as an academic.

—Sheila Seifert, instructor, Community College of Denver

believe that abortion should be a woman's right have started to wonder out loud if there is a better way. Even former President Bill Clinton, who has championed abortion rights, said in a now famous phrase that abortion should be "safe, legal, and rare."

It might be fair to say that no issue in our day has elicited so much passion as abortion. But it seems to me that there is only one real issue, and that is this: When does life begin?

So when does life begin? Scripture teaches that life begins before birth. Psalm 139:13 is perhaps the most famous, but by no means the only, passage that makes this point: "For you created my inmost being; you knit me together in my mother's womb." Luke 1:44 says that John the Baptist "leaped for joy" in the womb at the sound of Mary's voice.

Scripture is clear that life begins before birth, but does it begin at conception? This is a much tougher theological and ethical question. Let me just say I believe it does, and the great thinkers of the Christian tradition have always held this to be so.

If you or someone you know has had an abortion or is pregnant and considering abortion, Focus on the Family (www.family.org) has biblical resources that will foster spiritual healing for post-abortion grief and help women and men understand the importance of the sanctity of life and protecting the unborn. If you or someone you know is pregnant and considering an abortion, contact this pro-family organization by calling 1-800-A-FAMILY (232-6459) during business hours (Mountain Time) and ask to speak to a counselor.

Pornography

The word *pornography* comes from the Greek *porneia, porneuo,* and *porne.* These words appear many times in Scripture, though they are not translated into English as "pornography." *Porneia* is translated "fornication" in the King James Version (Matthew 5:32; John 8:41; Romans 1:29; and elsewhere). *Porneuo* is the verb "to commit fornication," as in 1 Corinthians 6:18. *Porne* is translated "harlot" in Matthew 21:31-32; 1 Corinthians 6:15; and Revelation 17:5.

Adding the suffixes *-graph* or *-graphy* adds the meaning "to write," though now it applies to photography and video as well. Therefore, pornography would be the writing down or the visual representation of fornication or harlotry.

Even without all that, however, Scripture is clear that we should engage in no activity that incites us to lust. Matthew 5:28, for example, says "that anyone who looks at a woman lustfully has already committed adultery with her in his heart." Psalm 101:3 also sets a high standard: "I will set before my eyes no vile thing."

Alex on His Soapbox

Don't win the intellectual battle but lose the moral battle. I had two friends in college, Matt and Kristin, whom I looked up to. They were the "perfect" Christian couple. They would often go to Matt's apartment near campus. Kristin would come over because she loved his CD collection. They would listen to music and talk for hours. They even had their quiet times together. But soon the time they had reserved for devotions became quiet time for sex. Ultimately, the stereo and CD collection that they had enjoyed so much was sold to a pawn shop in order to pay for Kristin's abortion.

Matt told me later, "If someone had said that this would be my college experience, I would have said he was crazy. But it happened so gradually."

The Bible says a man should "take heed lest he fall" (1 Corinthians 10:12, KJV).

So even though the English word *pornography* is not in Scripture, it seems inconceivable to me that these passages and many more do not refer directly to modern pornography. Indeed, I have rarely met anyone—not the most hardened atheists or the most ardent free-speech advocates—who will admit that *all* forms of pornography are okay. Even those who place no stock in God's Word will, ironically, usually admit that certain forms of pornography are disgusting, are degrading, and should be illegal. Even "culture warriors" who disagree about abortion and homosexuality will often agree about pornography—though sometimes for different reasons. Non-Christians will often say it is degrading to women and therefore violates their notions of pluralism. Christians believe it is immoral because it is prohibited by God, it incites lust, and it leads to other sins. It is highly addicting and has the potential to destroy relationships and marriages. Many companies, Christian as well as secular, will terminate employees on the spot who are found to have pornography on their office computers.

For all of the above reasons, let's agree on this: Pornography is bad, and we should give no place for it in our lives.

Homosexuality

Next to abortion, homosexuality has become perhaps the most emotionally charged issue of our time.

Make no mistake about it: Homosexual behavior is a clear violation of God's Word. But Christians have focused on politics and science—Is homosexuality genetic or learned?—and every other way of talking about homosexuality except the one way that makes sense theologically and philosophically, and that is to say that heterosexual, monogamous marriage between one man and one woman is the way God planned for sex to be employed and enjoyed. (For more, see chapter 10 and question 13 in appendix I.)

Overheard in the Student Lounge

In my freshman-level sociology class we took a field trip to a porn shop. We had to do a scavenger hunt, and the professor handed out lists of what we were supposed to find. The list included both types of porn (homosexual and heterosexual), an X-rated video, various sensual toys, condoms, and things so out there I won't even write about them. We were assigned a report on "butt plugs" and how keeping them in your body was an exercise in self-discipline. It was just a basic sociology class, required on my course syllabus. But the classroom experience just included so much shocking stuff.

A person who had undergone a sex change came as guest lecturer to inform about "the other 2 percent of the population" who supposedly want to get a sex change. Also, an admitted pedophile came in to share his story.

I told the professor that I didn't want to go into the porn shop, and I didn't want to have to write the paper from the items on the scavenger hunt. The professor told me that my "sheltered" upbringing had made me hypersensitive, afraid, and biased against things that I didn't understand. He reminded me that this class was required and that I must fulfill its requirements in order to eventually graduate.

What I was exposed to was awful, and I hated having things in my mind that I found to be so offensive. The porn was really like mental poison. But I just had to get through it, though it was really disturbing.

—*Jeffrey C., Arizona*

Gambling

Even people on opposite sides of the political spectrum can often agree that gambling is bad. Though gambling is not explicitly condemned in Scripture, most theologians and biblical scholars of all stripes agree that biblical commands not to covet have application to gambling.

There is also the important biblical idea that we should depend on God for our needs, not a quick fix at the casino. And while God can and sometimes does provide for our needs supernaturally, or through the generosity of others, God's primary way for us to make money is by our work. "If a man will not work, he shall not eat" (2 Thessalonians 3:10). Proverbs 13:11 is also instructive on this point: "Dishonest money dwindles away, but he who gathers money little by little makes it grow."

Of course, advocates of gambling say that it is not dishonest money. "You pays your money and you takes your chances," as the old carnival barker used to say. Sometimes you win, and sometimes you lose. Either way, you get some entertainment value, some thrill, from the experience. That's why the industry doesn't even call it gambling; they call it "gaming."

But that's exactly the problem. The thrill of gambling, like the thrill of pornography, can become consuming. Lotteries, which were illegal in almost every state just 25 years ago, are now legal in 44 states. Study after study has shown that those who can least afford to gamble are those most likely to do so.[4]

Gambling is becoming a bigger problem on college campuses. A 1995 survey of 1,200 students on two Minnesota universities found that nearly 90 percent had gambled at least once in the past 12 months. In 2003, the National Collegiate Athletic Association (NCAA) conducted a survey of 21,000 student athletes and found that gambling was rampant. Not only did more than 70 percent admit to gambling in the past year, 20 percent of the men and 5 percent of the women said they had bet on NCAA sports, even though they would be banned for life if caught![5]

Gambling is rampant. Gambling is an addiction. Gambling is destructive. If you've never gambled, don't start. If you are "dabbling" in it by buying an occasional lottery ticket, stop before it gets out of control.

Materialism

Materialism, as you might guess, means the pursuit of material things.

College campuses have a complex relationship with materialism. On the one hand, there is a strong strain of antimaterialism on college

By the Book

There is a way that seems right to a man, but in the end it leads to death.

—*Proverbs 14:12*

■ ■ ■

Resolved, never to do anything which I should be afraid to do if it were the last hour of my life.

—*Jonathan Edwards, American preacher, theologian and missionary (1703–1758)*[6]

■ ■ ■

The Christian ideal has not been tried and found wanting; it has been found difficult and left untried.

—*G. K. Chesterton, British writer and Christian apologist (1874–1936)*[7]

campuses. You can still find 1960s-style hippies on or near many college campuses. And, of course, the nature of college itself tends to create a kind of class leveling on campus.

But the accumulation of material wealth is not what God is calling us to. The purpose of your education is not to get a high-paying job. Wealth and a high-paying job may come to you, but it should never be your first priority. To quote Jesus on this topic: "Seek first his kingdom and his righteousness, and all these things will be given to you as well" (Matthew 6:33). Jesus also said that it is impossible to serve both "God and Money" (Matthew 6:24).

Having money is not bad. Worshiping it is idolatry. When our lives are organized around the accumulation and hoarding of wealth, we are worshiping a false god.

Hedonism

At its most basic level, hedonism is the pursuit of pleasure. Indeed, the Greek word *hedone* means "pleasure." It is a word usually associated with sexual pleasure.

Though materialism and hedonism are different in some important characteristics, I have lumped them together here because they both represent the same modern philosophy, perhaps best summed up in a country song by Toby Keith, "It's all about me!"

Because I spend an entire chapter on sexual purity (chapter 10), I will not dwell much on hedonism here except to say that the pleasure of sexual gratification is a cheap substitute for the true pleasure and joy of knowing God in an intimate way. The Westminster Catechism, which is a series of questions and answers about the essentials of the Christian faith, has as its first question: "What is the chief end of man?" The answer: "To know God and enjoy Him forever."

Jesus understood this when He said, "Just as the Son of Man did not come to be served, but to serve, and to give his life as a ransom for many" (Matthew 20:28). Jesus knew His purpose was not "all about me" but "all about God." He knew God's purpose for His life, and He fulfilled it, at the price of extreme pain. That example is the best argument against hedonism that I know.

Arming Yourself for Battle

This is indeed a spiritual battle. Did you know that the Bible has more than 300 references to battle, war, and warfare? Many of these refer specifically to spiritual warfare. I believe that God put so many references to war in the Bible because He knows the reality of the situation: We are in a life-and-death struggle with evil and the evil one.

But there is good news. We have powerful spiritual weapons. Regular Bible study, prayer, and other disciplines that will ensure your emotional, physical, and spiritual health will all yield good results in this arena. As Paul told the Corinthians, "The weapons we fight with are not the weapons of the world. On the contrary, they have divine power to demolish strongholds" (2 Corinthians 10:4). Prayer and the study of God's Word are two of the most powerful tools we have. Engage in them as if your spiritual life depends on them, because it does!

But there is one more thing I want you to consider that is not a part of the "normal" arsenal of spiritual weapons but is found throughout Scripture and is a vital part of spiritual battle: an accountability partner.

We all want someone who can "watch our backs," don't we? Fighter pilots have a wingman. Batman had Robin. In Scripture, David had Jonathan. Even Jesus had His "inner circle" of Peter, James, and John. Indeed, John is sometimes referred to as the disciple whom Jesus loved.

An accountability partner is someone who knows you—and to

whom you can tell everything, and I do mean everything. But more to the point, he or she is someone who will not let you get away with *not* telling everything. An accountability partner is someone who will ask you tough questions. Did you go on a date last night? Your accountability partner will ask if you did anything you shouldn't have done. Was your roommate out of town for the weekend? Your accountability partner will ask if you spent time on Internet sites you shouldn't have been to. Finding and becoming an accountability partner is not easy. A great accountability partner is someone who also wants an accountability partner, is not necessarily your best friend, offers absolute confidentiality, knows no reasonable question is off-limits, and makes a firm agreement for a fixed period of time.

There are all kinds of great benefits to having an accountability partner. An accountability partner really gets to know you, and you get to know him. Having a friend like that is rare indeed. When you fall, or are tempted to fall, an accountability partner can help pick you up and give you encouragement. And, to be honest, just knowing that you will have to face your accountability partner can keep you out of trouble. If you know that your accountability partner is going to ask you about every detail of this weekend's date with your boyfriend, you'd better believe that that will have an impact on your behavior.

EVERYTEEN Cameron

Of course, some people don't want accountability. Cameron didn't have time for church or Christian clubs. He was too busy getting involved in academic clubs, where he found approval. He tried calling his youth pastor back home to ask about homosexuality, but by then, Cameron had pretty much decided he could figure out this college adventure on his own and didn't really listen. After all, he was a smart guy.

If Cameron had been relentless in seeking out Christian fellowship and accountability in the first six months of school, his story might have been different. The attacks on the biblical pillars of morality might have been defused, and, instead of having his faith watered down, he could have gotten into studying the Bible and found refreshment in rivers of living water.

Chapter 8

Disciplines for Your Mind

I long to see you so that I may impart to
you some spiritual gift to make you **strong**.
—*Romans 1:11*

It's important to remember that when you're in high school and college, school is your job. Think of your report card as a paycheck.
Every A is a bonus, one that could save you thousands of dollars in
grad school fees because it will make you eligible for scholarships. Or
A's can pay off in better job opportunities when you graduate. It's a
mental matter, and with the right amount of discipline, you can succeed at getting good grades. But with the intense competition in your
classes, what will it take to succeed in academics? In life?

In chapter 4, we discussed physical disciplines, and I introduced
to you the "Mr. Miyagi Method." You remember: "Wax on, wax off."
The young "karate kid" was learning martial arts even though he
thought he was just waxing cars.

Two Frogs in a Bucket

There's an old story about two frogs that fall into a bucket of milk. The
straight, slick sides of the bucket make it impossible for the frogs to
crawl out, so they "froggy paddle" in the bucket until one frog can't go

on any longer and sinks beneath the frothy white surface of the milk. Just seconds after the first frog disappears, something remarkable happens. All that "frog-paddling" turned the milk to butter, and the second frog stands on the surface of the butter and hops out of the bucket.

Sometimes learning is that way. Stories about "genius" often focus on the moment of inspiration. They ignore the many hours of perspiration that preceded it. You may have heard the story about Alexander Graham Bell's invention of the telephone. The culmination came at a moment when Bell said to his assistant, "Mr. Watson, come here. I need you." What most accounts leave out are the two years of nonstop hard work that Bell had devoted to trial and error. Another

By the Book

No discipline seems pleasant at the time, but painful. Later on, however, it produces a harvest of righteousness and peace for those who have been trained by it.

—Hebrews 12:11

■ ■ ■

Therefore, prepare your minds for action; be self-controlled; set your hope fully on the grace to be given you when Jesus Christ is revealed.

—1 Peter 1:13

■ ■ ■

Seek freedom and become captive of your desires. Seek discipline and find your liberty.

—Frank Herbert, science fiction writer (1920–1986)[1]

famous story of intellectual breakthrough is the discovery of the double-helix structure for DNA, a discovery that revolutionized molecular biology. The folk tale is that codiscoverer Francis Crick was thinking about the problem when he dozed off, and somewhere between consciousness and sleep he dreamed of the structure.

The truth was much more mundane. Crick and his partner, James Watson, had been working on the problem for years. With the help of collaborator Rosalind Franklin and others, and through a laborious process of trial and error, Crick and Watson came to the right answer. Crick later said the discovery was "a series of blunders where we gradually found what the mistakes were."[2]

That's why this chapter will talk about the "boring" things like study habits, because, to quote Thomas Edison, "Genius is 1 percent inspiration and 99 percent persperation."[3]

EVERYTEENS Adam and Erin

Adam went to the academic dean for advice after the first-semester grades came in and he had a 2.0. The news wasn't good. He would have to earn a 3.75 this semester and gather three letters of recommendation from his professors to receive more scholarship money for his sophomore year. At the end of the meeting, Adam vowed to do better the next semester. How he would hate to go home and face his father, knowing he had failed to meet his expectations.

During the first few weeks in January, Adam put in some serious studying, a lot of it during chapel service. He aced the exams in all but one class. He turned in extra credit for chemistry. But by late January, the work was getting old. He discovered he could buy notes from students who had made A's the previous semester, and so he started skipping the boring classes like history and systematic theology.

One Saturday as he was walking to the library to study, a friend in a nearby dorm caught up to him on the sidewalk and invited him to come to a football playoff game party with some buddies.

■ ■ ■

Erin recovered from mono slowly. She cut back on all her activities except for a small Bible study that met in the dorm lounge on Thursday nights. She took a digital recorder to class and then downloaded the lectures onto her iPod. She reviewed any complicated lectures as she walked around campus or worked out in the weight room. Even though she was still always tired, she would lie awake wondering if all this work was worth it. She had one particularly difficult weekend after a physics exam. She knew she had blown it, because she had left the last two questions blank.

That night, she went with her roommate to her first party on campus and started to drink.

With All You're Getting, Get Wisdom

Learning is not a mechanical process. Hard work matters, and it matters a great deal. But so do rest and reflection. Study time is when you accumulate the building blocks of great ideas. The time of reflection is when you begin to understand how these building blocks fit together. I think that's why the Bible tells us to study, pray, proclaim, and serve—but when it comes to knowing God, the Bible has an odd instruction for us: "Be still, and know that I am God" (Psalm 46:10).

And it is that knowledge, the knowledge of God, that is the most important knowledge of all. The Bible uses the word *wisdom* to describe the highest form of learning. The poetic language of Proverbs often uses the words *wisdom* and *understanding* interchangeably, using both words in the same sentence for emphasis and dramatic effect. One of my favorite verses does just that. "Wisdom is supreme; there-

fore get wisdom. Though it cost all you have, get understanding"
(Proverbs 4:7).

Wisdom includes the knowledge of God, and it also includes the
idea of having the "mind of Christ" (1 Corinthians 2:16) as we look
out at the world. In other words, learning is more than just the accumulation of data or even the compiling of that data into some sort of
a knowledge base. It is having a perspective across time and space. It is
why we study history and languages in addition to science and math.

But most of all, the purpose of learning science and math and history is so that we can develop the tools of learning. The ultimate goals
are to become a lifelong learner and to learn well those things that are
most important—the things of God.

Humility

Scripture teaches that humility should be a way of life for the Christian: "Clothe yourselves with humility . . . because, 'God opposes the
proud but gives grace to the humble' " (1 Peter 5:5). The reason is

Overheard in the Student Lounge

My pastor once told me that if I wanted to know what kind of
person I would be in four years, I should look at the material I
was reading right then. If you want to be standing strong at the
end of four years, you must maintain a consistent time of reading and studying God's Word and meditating on it. If you want
to be a Romans 12:2 Christian who is transformed by the
renewing of your mind, make sure you are filling it with the
right stuff.

—Michael E., University of North Carolina, Asheville

simple: We are all made in God's image, and God made each of us special and unique. No matter how smart you are, you can learn something from the lowliest person on the planet. Someone once asked Mother Teresa how she maintained her humility as she became more famous and why she continued to serve the poorest of the poor in Calcutta, India. She said that she did not even consider thinking of herself as being better than those she served, because when she looked at the diseased, the poor, and the broken, she said she saw Jesus "in His distressing disguise."[4]

Humility is also that quality that says, "I'm not too proud to work hard." Humility is the mother of diligence and perseverance, both of which are essential to developing disciplines of the mind.

So, if you're not too proud to study, here are a few thoughts that will make that study time more effective and efficient.

Study habits

When it comes to study habits, the most important piece of advice I can give I already mentioned in chapter 4—and that is to schedule your study time and stick to that study schedule every day. But let me hit you with a few more tips that I have found work for me and for some of the most successful students I've run across in 20 years of working with scholars at all levels.

Review your notes every day. Today, Dr. Marvin Royster has a successful orthopedic surgery practice in Atlanta and is also part of the medical staff for the Atlanta Braves. But 25 years ago he was a straight-A chemistry major at the University of Georgia. Dr. Royster used to say he was not brilliant, though most of his friends would disagree. But he worked hard. Every day after class he would come back to his dorm room and copy all of his notes for the day—in every class. He said doing that disciplined him to review his notes while the information was still fresh.

"If I didn't understand it then," he said, "there was no way I would understand it six weeks later, when I would be tested on it." If there was anything in his notes he didn't understand, he would ask his professor for clarification the next day. "When it came time to study for a test," he said, "my notes were neat and organized, and I understood the material. I didn't have to cram for exams, because I learned the material as I went along."

Ask questions in class. In most classes, knowledge builds upon knowledge. You learn to multiply after you've mastered addition. You learn algebra after you've mastered multiplication. You learn to write research papers after you've mastered shorter essays. What that means is that if you don't master the building block skills and knowledge,

A Word from the Faculty

"Do the extra credit"—Not only is the extra credit usually an easy way to improve your grade, it is also usually the shortest path to finding out what makes your professor tick. Professors usually assign extra-credit projects or activities that are of interest to them. It might involve attending a lecture or reading a certain book. But you may be sure that if the professor makes this extra credit available, it's because he knows that it may not fit the core learning objectives of the class, but he's interested personally.

—*Anonymous*

you'll be lost when it comes to the advanced skills and knowledge. By reviewing your notes every day, you can know immediately if you understand a basic concept. If you just don't get it, ask your professor for clarification immediately. You will get the clarification you need to stay up with the material, and your professor will be pleased that you are truly engaged with the material—even outside of class.

Turn off your iPod. I must confess that this tip might say more about me than about solid research. The truth is that the research is mixed on whether background music helps or hurts the study process. Maybe it's because I'm a musician, but I can't listen to music passively. If the music is any good, you're inclined to more actively listen. When I try to read or study with music playing, I generally find that my retention of one or the other—either the music or the material I'm studying—is diminished. So here's my advice: Turn the music off and reward yourself with the music when the studying is done.

Get plenty of sleep before tests. I'm always amazed when I hear about students who pull all-nighters before exams—and then wonder why they did so poorly. To begin with, study marathons have diminishing returns. The research is absolutely convincing on this point. Unless you are an extraordinarily unusual student, a couple of hours of uninterrupted study time are about all you can stand before you need to do something else for a while. That's especially true when you're tired. Studies have shown that when you drive when you're sleepy, your awareness and reaction time are as bad as that of a drunk driver. How effective do you think it is to study when you're drunk? The answer is not very. The effective student will keep up in class and schedule a few extra hours of study time in the final days before tests—and then get a good, full night's sleep before the test. In most cases, an extra hour of sleep is more than worth an hour of missed sleepy-headed study.

Great books

If we lived in a world where the *-isms* we covered in chapter 5 were not rampant on the college campus, I wouldn't have to tell you what I'm about to tell you next. But the fact is that the world is as it is, so we have to deal with it.

What I mean is this: It is possible, even probable, that you will make it through four years of college and not be truly educated in the great ideas of Western civilization or in the Judeo-Christian tradition.

That's why I recommend that you get yourself a list of the great books of Western civilization and make reading through it a lifelong pursuit. Books like Bunyan's *Pilgrim's Progress* or Dante's *Inferno* offer powerful insights into Christian thought and into the human condition. George Orwell's *1984* or Aldous Huxley's *Brave New World* dramatize the destructive power of *-isms*. Indeed, Shakespeare and the King James Version of the Bible influenced much of the literature written in the past 400 years.

Of course, knowing what the great books are is something of a challenge. That is why I have my own rather subjective list at the end of this book. Start there, or start somewhere else, but start soon, and continue with it for a lifetime. That's how you make your education complete.

It's All One!

Now, all of this study advice might not sound like the kind of hyper-spiritual, theologically deep insight you might expect from a seminary president, but I want you to understand that I consider studying to develop the intellect to be a sacred, God-ordained activity. Scripture tells us, "Do your best to present yourself to God as one approved, a workman who does not need to be ashamed and who correctly handles the word of truth" (2 Timothy 2:15). Jesus was described by Luke as a young man who "grew in wisdom and stature, and in favor with God and men" (2:52). Let me put it plainly: We rarely follow Jesus more closely than when we develop our intellect—that unique ability God gives us to discern His glory both in His world and in His creation.

That may sound like quite a lot to get out of something so mundane as copying your notes at the end of the day, but it's as true as anything you'll read in this book.

EVERYTEENS Adam and Erin

At first Adam said no to the party, but then he reconsidered. *I'll just go for a half hour—everyone needs a break now and again.* For the rest of the semester he played the grade game—seeing how little work he could actually do and still make 94 percent. He won the game but lost

---

Alex on His Soapbox

Learn all that you can at college. But in doing so, don't forget to think for yourself. Don't assume that you are obligated to accept something just because it was said by a professor. The importance of critical thinking and discernment is echoed in these words from a great Christian thinker of the past: "Without education, we are in a horrible and deadly danger of taking educated people seriously" (G. K. Chesterton, 1874–1936).[5]

the scholarship battle. He could find only one teacher to write him a recommendation. The others looked at their grade books and declined to support him since his attendance had been so sporadic.

■ ■ ■

Erin left the party early. The half can of beer had made her depressed instead of helping her relax. She felt guilty because in her Bible study—or was it during her Bible readings?—she had recently read, "Do not get drunk on wine. . . . Instead, be filled with the Spirit" (Ephesians 5:18). She went home lonely and depressed and feeling like a social failure, but she was still sober.

During her next physics lab, she received her exam back. She had earned a B+ on the curve. The T.A. told her that was the toughest exam she'd see all year and that she had done well, especially considering she'd left two questions blank. Elated, she went back to her studies with renewed vigor. She went back to her Bible study with profound thankfulness.

Part 3

A Significant Life

One thing God has spoken,
two things have I heard:
that you, O God, are **strong**,
and that you, O Lord, are loving.
Surely you will reward each person
according to what he has done.
—*Psalm 62:11-12*

The pressure to conform to the thinking of the world is enormous. In the mid 1970s, a Christian Ph.D. student was with a colleague from Michigan State University when the latter started scoffing at some of the claims of Scripture. Creation. Stories of people living 900 or more years. Miracles. He turned to the Christian grad student and asked, "Do you really believe all that stuff?"

Today, the student recalls, "I couldn't believe the single word coming out of my mouth. I didn't want to sound simplistic or ignorant. So I said, 'No.' I failed to affirm that these stories were true. They were perhaps myths, or metaphors."

The grad student remembers that moment with great regret: "It pains me to say that this one time, I caved. But that's the power of academic peer pressure."

Today Gary Habermas, Ph.D., is known as one of the world's top scholars on the resurrection and historical evidence for Jesus. He has let me tell this story so others will see that the time to prepare for the lions' den is before you're thrown to the lions. Be prayed up and studied up. You can be courageous when courage is required, but you have to prepare in advance.

I also tell this story so you can revel in the ending. God uses "failures" to do His work. In fact, that's the only kind He uses. Remember Jacob's lies? Moses' murder? David's adultery with Bathsheba? Peter's denial? Paul's persecution of the believers? Mark's desertion of Paul when the Christian life got too tough?

God turned those people around and used their lives in significant ways despite their sins. Jacob became the father of the nation Israel. Moses led the Israelites out of Egypt. David was a great king and a man "after [God']s own heart" (1 Samuel 13:14). Peter preached after the resurrection and saw thousands come to Christ. Paul became a great apostle. Mark lived to write a gospel account.

Even if you fail or have down times, don't give up. Everyone will fail. But God can and will and is waiting to redeem your life. The prophet Jeremiah, who was speaking for God, said it somewhat differently. "For I know the plans I have for you, . . . plans to prosper you and not to harm you, plans to give you hope and a future" (29:11) This beautiful passage tells us that not only is it possible for our lives to have significance, God Himself has a plan for us!

But what does that plan look like? How can you have significance?

Chapter 9

Ethics

I write to you . . . because you are **strong**,
and the word of God lives in you,
and you have overcome the evil one.

—1 John 2:14

One of the great themes of Western literature is the fall of the mighty. In the tragedies of Shakespeare we can hear the laments of Richard III and King Lear, who are both brought low by circumstances and their foolish pride. We remember an even earlier tale, the great warrior hero Achilles from *The Iliad*, whose only weakness results in his death. But perhaps nowhere has this idea been more passionately expressed than by the famous lament of David in 2 Samuel 1:19: "Your glory, O Israel, lies slain on your heights. How the mighty have fallen!"

In modern times, we have the examples of President Richard Nixon saying, "I am not a crook," as the extent of his crookedness was being made known. President Bill Clinton's dalliance with an intern nearly cost him his presidency, and it did tarnish his effectiveness and his legacy. WorldCom, Enron: These corporate scandals resulted in prison, suicide, dishonor, and financial ruin for many.

And it is too easy to say that these lapses in behavior were committed by men who didn't have Christian beliefs. For one thing, many of the people in these scandals were or are professing Christians. And for another thing, it is not hard to look at the evangelical church and see a fair share of moral failures. Churches all across America have been ripped apart by sexual scandal. High profile cases have involved televangelists Jim Bakker and Jimmy Swaggart. More recently, mega-church pastor Ted Haggard disgraced his pulpit, which highlights the fact that while proper belief ("orthodoxy") is important, it is not enough. Proper behavior ("orthopraxy") is also required of Christians and leaders.

What we need, in other words, is a return to Christian ethics.

EVERYTEENS David and Cameron

Seems that digital technology has been helping students cheat on David's campus. It's rather easy to take a photo of an exam with a cell-phone camera. Certain of David's friends began helping him get the questions to tough exams. He started cheating in his humanities classes, telling himself that it didn't really matter because he had more time to study for accounting classes. In the long run, he'd be a better accountant, which was his main goal. His conscience bothered him at first, but the twinges were easy to ignore because his father applauded his good grades, and it took some of the academic pressure off.

■   ■   ■

Cameron didn't go home for Thanksgiving. Instead he went with Nolan and his friends to an out-of-state conference for gay and lesbian leaders. Looking back, Cameron isn't sure why he decided to have a homosexual encounter with Nolan, but it felt right, so important, so urgent at the time. Afterward, he could never look at himself in the same way again. His experience had left a mark on his life, a distinct before-and-after moment. In some ways he felt more connected to

Nolan than ever, and in another, so very alone. He knew that the Bible condemned what he had done, and for a while, he wondered if he had made a mistake. *But still,* he asked himself, *how could I have known if the gay lifestyle was right for me unless I tried it?*

What Are Ethics?

At its most basic level, ethics are the philosophies that govern the way we live our lives. The word *ethics* derives from the Greek word *ethike,* which means "the science of morals." Ethics are not just what we say or even what we believe—though both are very important. Ethics are what we habitually *do.*

Of course, the Bible says there is an intimate relationship between what we believe, say, and do. Jesus helped us see the close relationship

A Word from the Faculty

There is a tendency for freshmen to put their professors on pedestals, even if they do not realize they are doing so. Often-times, this can lead to students trusting the classroom agenda of professors, which can often extend beyond the formal sub-ject matter of the discipline into belief and lifestyle persuasions. I encourage students to remember to respect their professors but also to remember they should not base their own faith on the values projected from behind the lectern but from trusted sources they have known for more than just three hours a week for a semester.

—*Michael B. Ramey, Ph.D., Department of Chemistry,
Appalachian State University, North Carolina*

between our heart and our speech when He said, "For out of the overflow of the heart the mouth speaks" (Matthew 12:34). Given this relationship between our beliefs, our words, and our actions, we need to answer the question: What is a true Christian ethic?

I believe it is one in which our beliefs, words, and actions are in alignment, and they are all three based on the truth of Scripture.

The second question is: How do I make decisions about how to live my life on a daily basis? Before we answer that question, let's look at some tests or criteria *not* to use when making important life decisions.

Ethical Relativism

In chapter 5 we discussed relativism as a system of belief that says there is no absolute truth. Ethical relativism is the idea that there are no absolutely right or wrong behaviors. It all depends on the outcome you are hoping to produce. One form of ethical relativism is known as "situational ethics," which says that the situation dictates the behavior. Situational ethics is often popularly expressed by the saying, "The end justifies the means."

Situational ethics is not only tolerated, but often actively encouraged. In fact, in folk tales, we sometimes turn those who practice situational ethics into heroes. Robin Hood, for example, robbed from the rich and gave to the poor. Many of the so-called "antiheroes" of modern movies live by a code that is highly subjective and often outside of the moral, legal, and ethical standards of the conventional world. James Bond 007, Clint Eastwood's Dirty Harry, Neo from *The Matrix*—all these characters exercise some form of ethical relativism that viewers are expected to affirm and celebrate.

So it is no surprise that we are vulnerable to practicing ethical relativism or situational ethics in our own lives. A simple way to determine whether you are falling into the trap of ethical relativism is to be clear about *why* you are doing what you are doing. Are you doing it because of a clear instruction (either "for" or "against") from Scripture, or are you subjecting your actions to a different test?

The feelings test. Many people (even some Christians) have made feelings the ultimate standard for life. Actions are assumed to be okay as long as the behavior in question *feels* right. Personal preference is fine when ordering lunch or picking out clothes. But moral truth is in no way determined by feelings. The false assumption behind the feelings test is that changeable emotions are an accurate test for unchanging truth.

The authority figure test. Influence. Reputation. Honor. We've all been around people who are leaders. Certainly it is proper to show respect to persons of authority and to acknowledge the accomplishments of others. But all of the professors, teachers, elected officials, scientists—and even peers whose acceptance we crave—should not force us or even tempt us to accept things that we know are wrong.

Overheard in the Student Lounge

Select friends who will keep you accountable as well as encourage you morally and spiritually. These types of friends become an important support network as you are away from home. The right kinds of friends will become some of the most important and influential people in your life during the four (or more) years of college, and beyond.

—Julie, University of North Carolina, Chapel Hill

The pragmatics test. The word *pragmatic* simply means "practical." A pragmatic person wants to know what works or, to put it another way, what action or thing will yield the best result. There are a lot of things that result in "good" outcomes that are still wrong. Yeah, it would be pragmatic not to declare all my income for taxes so that I have more to pay for a friend's medical care, but it would still be ethically wrong—not to mention illegal.

The economics test. For some people, right and wrong cannot be decided until they see the "price tag." The opinion here is that something is right only if I think it is affordable. Should you pay back the

By the Book

When one door closes, another door opens, but we often look so long and so regretfully at the closed door that we do not see the one that has opened for us.

—*Alexander Graham Bell, scientist and inventor (1847–1922)*[1]

■ ■ ■

Do all the good you can, by all the means you can, in all the ways you can, in all the places you can, at all the times you can, to all the people you can, as long as ever you can.

—*John Wesley, English theologian (1703–1791)*[2]

■ ■ ■

Anyone . . . who knows the good he ought to do and doesn't do it, sins.

—*James 4:17*

friend who lent you some money, even though he has forgotten you owe it?

The popular opinion test. People of all ages struggle with this. Particularly in America, we tend to think that the majority rules. Sometimes we say, "If everyone is doing it, it can't be wrong!" Well, *wrong!*

The age test. Here is where Christian values have possibly suffered the most. Some say that the Bible may be a moral guidebook, but what it says is old-fashioned. After all, it was written thousands of years ago. What is right, however, is still right.

The reputation test. I also call this the Ego Protection Test. It's true that the Bible says a "good name" is better than great riches (Proverbs 22:1). But too often we don't want to *be* good, but only *appear* good. When we do the right thing, we don't have to worry about our reputation. It takes care of itself.

The autonomy test. Situations may prompt our autonomous side to cry out, "I am free to do whatever I want, whenever I want."

Classical Ethical Concepts

Even without the instruction of Scripture, wise men and women have realized that ethical standards are essential to the proper operating of culture and society.

Aristotle (384–322 B.C.) wrote several works of ethics, but the most famous one has come to be known as the *Nicomachean Ethics*. This treatise was either written for, or edited by, Aristotle's son Nicomachus, and it was intended to be an instruction from an older man to a younger one about how the younger man should live. Aristotle praised what he called a "golden mean," which was behavior between an excess of a certain quality and a deficiency in that quality.

For example, it is good to be thrifty, because an absence of thrift results in profligacy (extravagance or licentiousness); however, an excess of thrift results in stinginess or miserliness. The golden mean is to live between stinginess and profligacy.

There is much wisdom in Aristotle's *Nicomachean Ethics*. In fact, of the two great philosophers of the ancient world, Aristotle and Plato, most Christians consider Aristotle to be the one most closely aligned with Christian thought. Most modern Catholic thinkers and many Protestant theologians believe that you can draw a more or less straight line from Aristotle to Saint Thomas Aquinas (1225–1274) to modern Christian apologetics and Christian worldview thinking.

Christian Ethics

While there is no single Christian ethic, it would be fair to say that Christian ethics are those behaviors the Bible says are good, and unethical behaviors are those behaviors the Bible condemns. As I suggested above, the *Nicomachean Ethics* could be reduced to a list of "golden means" that on one side had deficiencies and on the other side had excesses. In that tradition, Christian thinkers compiled their own lists of the "seven deadly sins" and the "seven virtues." The seven deadly sins are lust, gluttony, greed, sloth, wrath, envy, and pride. The seven virtues are chastity, abstinence, liberality (generosity), diligence, patience, kindness, and humility. And though the seven sins and the seven virtues are opposites, there is no golden mean between them. Humility is a virtue and pride is a sin. The goal is to be humble and not proud. Being halfway between humility and pride is no virtue.

But perhaps the most important aspect of Christian ethics is the "doing of the thing." In other words, it is not enough to extol virtue. One must actually be virtuous.

EVERYTEENS Cameron and David

Both David and Cameron made ethical choices based on what they wanted to do instead of what they knew was right. For David, cheating was practical and popular, so he did it. He didn't hold himself up to the standards of integrity he had been taught. Cameron knew that

Alex on His Soapbox

In most American colleges, earning a degree in business now involves taking a course or two in ethics. Since 2001, the requirement to take at least one course in ethics is up by 20 percent in college business-degree programs. Technological advances of recent years have created new opportunities for workplace crime, and so-called white-collar crimes bring a renewed need for the study of ethics.

The renewed emphasis on ethical studies comes from the Association to Advance Collegiate Schools of Business, a world-recognized board of accreditation. "This [ethics] is, without question, their major interest in the twenty-first century so far," says Dr. Pat Raines, dean of the business school at Belmont's Massey Graduate School of Business in Tennessee.

The call for ethical awareness, ethical behavior, and "social responsibility" is interesting in light of the political correctness, pluralism, and moral relativism assumed by most schools.[3]

what he was doing went against the Bible also, but he felt he had to try it for himself. Not seeking the shelter of biblical wisdom, David and Cameron opened themselves up to a lifestyle of seeming self-gratification but that would eventually lead to spiritual turmoil.

Ethics on the College Campus

So what do you do with all of that? The answer to that question is up to you. I wanted to share all of that history and all of those tests with you for a specific reason. I did not want to confuse you, and I certainly didn't want to bore you. But I did want you to come to a particular conclusion. I am hoping you are now saying to yourself, "You know, this matter of ethics can be complicated, but I think I can cut through all the complexity by simply adhering to the highest ethical standards possible."

So set a high standard for yourself, pray without ceasing, choose wisely, and humbly repent when you choose badly. The result of all of this will be a college experience that will have an impact on your life and the lives of others—for all eternity.

Chapter 10

Sexual Purity

He will keep you **strong** to the end,
so that you will be blameless on the
day of our Lord Jesus Christ.
—*1 Corinthians 1:8*

Sex.

I know I already have your attention with that one word, so I won't need a better introduction than that. And that's why even though an endless stream of books has been written about the subject, I believe it is important that we look at this issue squarely from a biblical perspective, even to the point of confronting some uncomfortable issues that you may not hear anywhere else.

But before we do that, let's check in again with Megan.

EVERYTEEN Megan

Megan, you may remember from chapter 3, was struggling with loneliness while living on a large campus. In high school she had been known as "the smart girl," and that was a label she liked. But college was a completely different experience for Megan. She chose a large school that was known for its science, math, and engineering programs.

At this school, everyone was smart—a lot of them were what she called "scary smart." She thought she didn't have time to join a church or seek out a Christian group on campus because she had to study so much. She began spending a lot of time with John, a non-Christian study partner, and before she knew it, she was emotionally attached to him but lacked the emotional fortitude to walk away from the rela-

Overheard in the Student Lounge

In a class on human sexuality, we were constantly told that AIDS was the fault of conservative rich people, who, out of greed, did not care that people die. We were told again and again that politically conservative people could have stopped AIDS during the 1980s, but they wouldn't.

Part of my art class involved going to an art fair. But when we got there, it was an art fair that was exclusively about porn. Every project had to relate somehow to human sexuality. There were also pictures and "creations" about cutting, flailing, and things that were, well, just revolting. There were even people giving speeches about porn, politics, and having a Q&A about porn, complete with video clips. We had to stay there for about four hours.

I had chosen this undergraduate art class as an elective. I had always liked drawing and thought, "Hey, I'll at least learn some of the basics." What I learned was that supposedly, sex is an obsession for everyone and that people use the powers of sex and politics to control other people. I guess I'll learn drawing some other time.

—Drew, Arizona

tionship when it started to get out of hand. She was in the stronghold of an emotional trap.

That much I told you earlier. Here's the rest of the story.

With football season over, winter weekends on big college campuses can be quiet. For those with a well-balanced life and friends, these days of emotional stillness can be blessings, real gifts. But Megan didn't experience them this way. The only relief from her loneliness was her study group, which had formed when they had taken chemistry together. In the new semester, though, the only person in the study group who still had a class with Megan was John. So Megan and John continued to get together two or sometimes three evenings a week to study at the library. Because it was just the two of them now, and Megan didn't like walking alone across campus in the dark, John would often walk her back to her dorm.

Men on the hall, especially on the weekends, were common. This particular winter evening, Megan's roommate was out of town, and John went upstairs to Megan's room. Before the end of the evening they were making out on Megan's bed. They did not have sex that night, but before too many weeks went by they did. Both were virgins until then, so for both Megan and John this was a monumental event. They had never talked about marriage, or even if they were boyfriend and girlfriend. But they both knew that something more than a physical union had occurred.

Everyone's Not Doing It—But Most Are

First of all, let's acknowledge that what happened to Megan is not that uncommon among young people who as teenagers attend good churches, go on youth retreats, and do all the programs we put youth through in today's evangelical churches—including abstinence training.

According to Lauren Winner in her book *Real Sex: The Naked Truth About Chastity,* "About 65 percent of America's teens have sex by the time they finish high school, and teenage 'dating' websites . . . encourage teenage patrons to select not prom dates but partners for casual sex."[1]

We live in a culture that encourages premarital and extramarital sexual activity. And we must also say that the church's attempts to counteract this tendency have largely been unsuccessful.

That's why I thought it would be instructive to look at Megan's example. For Megan, a relationship with John was an antidote to loneliness. And for both of them, sex became an emotional point of

Alex on His Soapbox

Get married? Are you kidding? I'm nowhere near ready to get married.

You may be saying that now, but the time will come soon enough when you'll start thinking about it. And as I have been through the process myself and seen thousands of young people wrestle with the question, I'm always amazed at some of the reasons people get married—or don't get married. I've heard people say:

- I'm going to wait until I finish college (or graduate school).
- I want to travel before I settle down.
- I want to marry my best friend.

Don't get me wrong; I have nothing against finishing college, traveling, or marrying your best friend. I did all three! I will say, however, that making a decision like marriage based on these considerations is like choosing a life preserver based on its

no return. Though they couldn't say what had happened when they had sex that first time, sex joined them in a way that they could not easily ignore. Because both of them had been virgins, and Megan knew the gnawing guilt and subsequent shame that she had done something wrong, they thought that becoming boyfriend and girlfriend would become a way to make it right.

Shame and Guilt

That gnawing guilt Megan experienced is that feeling God allows us to have when we have broken His law. Theologically speaking, "guilt"

color. A colorful life preserver is fine, but I would be more interested in whether it floats! Here are a few, somewhat better reasons to get married:

- You've found a life partner who shares your passion and calling in life.
- You have the same beliefs, values, and goals.
- You are ready to have children.

I would add, for the man in the relationship, that he should be prepared to financially support the new household.

Even within the church, that third point is a bit controversial. But make no mistake about it: In God's order of things, marriage is for procreation. In the normal course of things, the end result of sex is babies. Not all married couples can or will have children, but all married couples should be emotionally and spiritually prepared to have children. If you're not prepared to have children, you are not ready for marriage.

is the condition of violating the law. "Shame" is the emotion you feel when you have the knowledge of that guilt.

The truth is that Megan and John had violated one of God's most

A Word from the Faculty

When you're dating, consider this: Your future spouse will greatly appreciate it if you become the sort of person who can form deep friendships with and understand members of the opposite sex. He or she will not appreciate your having had multiple sexual partners. It's not merely disapproval; he or she might be harmed by whatever sexual past you've had.

Your past can create insecurities that might otherwise not be there; it can intrude on the intimacy of your marriage and deeply and adversely affect your sexual relationship with your spouse. Your spouse can wonder how he or she compares with your past partners, worry that you'll wistfully remember past experiences, fear that you have built habits of promiscuity that will later cause you to stray; and so on.

It's easy when you're young to discount these worries, but they are among the most painful struggles that couples can face in a marriage. It's also easy for Christian men in particular to turn to pornography and to think that they are somehow doing okay because they are "just looking" and not really having sex with other women. But pornography is addictive and destroys marriages, and the pain that couples go through in dealing with that issue is intense beyond what most college students could ever imagine.

—*Anonymous professor,*
University of Notre Dame, Indiana

fundamental laws for order in the universe He had created. Scripture speaks explicitly about sexuality and the proper relationship between men and women. To put it plainly, God gave us both our bodies and our sexual desires. But He allows us to satisfy these sexual desires only within the boundaries of marriage. Jesus said, "If you hold to my teaching, you are really my disciples. Then you will know the truth, and the truth will set you free" (John 8:31-32). You can't have true freedom without following God's ways. I believe that when you know the truth about creation and sexuality, obeying God's law becomes, not a burden, but a joy.

Two Become One

When God created man, He created the man in His image. God's decision to then make woman out of man's rib created a beautiful and powerful image for us—and gave us an important theological doctrine, the doctrine of complementarity. "*Complementarity*" is the idea that men and women complement each other. Note that I said *complement*, not *compliment* (though they should do that, too!).

In America, we value "rugged individualism." Even the U.S. Army had an advertising slogan that bragged, "An Army of One." The idea that I am not complete, that I need something or someone else, is almost abhorrent to the American psyche.

Of course, when the Bible talks about two becoming one, it is talking about much more than sex, but it is important that it is *also* talking about sex. Lauren Winner puts it memorably:

> In a graphic speech, Adam speaks of his and Eve's becoming one
> flesh. One-fleshness both is and is not metaphor. It captures an
> all-encompassing, overarching oneness—they marry, husband
> and wife enter an institution that points them toward familial,

domestic, emotional, and spiritual unity. But the one flesh of which Adam speaks is also overtly sexual, suggesting sexual intercourse, the only physical state other than pregnancy where it is hard to tell where one person's body stops and the other's starts.[2]

It is precisely this sort of "familial, domestic, emotional, and spiritual unity" that we all long for, and that is why the Christian concept that sex outside of marriage is wrong is not so much a restriction as it is a road sign pointing us in the right direction. The truth is that sex outside of marriage is a cheap imitation of the kind of physical and spiritual unity that God desires for us.

On a theological level, it is also important to remember that throughout Scripture the church is referred to as the "body of Christ" and the "bride of Christ." So even though it sounds jarring to say it so bluntly, it is both profound and theologically accurate to say that sex between a man and a woman within the boundaries of marriage—with its possibilities for both spiritual unity and physical fruitfulness—is the most accurate and complete picture we humans have of the Creator God at work in the world and of God's relationship, through His Son Jesus, with humankind.

All of this helps to explain why fornication and adultery—any form of sex outside of marriage—is so consistently condemned by Scripture. God is not a killjoy. Just the opposite. God wants our joy to be complete. Scriptural restrictions regarding sex are designed to protect us from what Winner calls the "faux sex that goes on outside marriage [that] is not really sex at all."[3]

Some Practical Advice

All of this is why I don't want to give you a list of do's and don'ts regarding sex. I've been around long enough to know that they rarely work, and, besides, there are already a lot of good lists out there.

But sometimes, in the "heat of the moment," it is good to have some guidelines that help you know what to do and give you the strength to do it. Here are a few ideas that have helped others, and they may help you too.

Sisters and brothers

Have you ever considered that your boyfriend (or girlfriend) is also your brother (or sister) in Christ and that you therefore have a responsibility to help with his or her spiritual maturity? The world tells us that relationships between the sexes should stir up arousal and personal satisfaction. Scripture gives us a message that is almost the opposite of that: "And let us consider how we may spur one another on toward love and good deeds" (Hebrews 10:24). The "love" that Scripture is referring to here is *agape* love—the selfless love that is best exemplified by Christ's love for the church. Indeed, it is not too much to say that if Christ's "job" while on earth was to reconcile us to God, then our relationship with our boyfriend or girlfriend, husband or wife, should have as its first priority their spiritual maturity.

What is and what is not sex?

Several years ago, President Bill Clinton made headlines by asserting that he "did not have sex with that woman." When all the facts came out, it turned out that a young intern had performed oral sex on him. But he steadfastly maintained that he had *not* had sexual relations with her.

Indeed, Clinton's attitude seems to be a majority position. Surveys indicate that as many as 55 percent of teenagers do not consider oral sex to be sex. But I would argue that Mrs. Clinton probably does not feel that way.

Neither does Scripture, and neither does author and college professor J. Budziszewski, who puts the matter plainly:

> The answer to the "'how far can I go?'" question has three parts: (1) You can't have sexual intercourse; (2) You can't do anything resembling sexual intercourse; and (3) You can't do anything that gets your motor running for sexual intercourse.[4]

Number 3 might require a bit of additional explanation. The Bible uses the word "lust" to describe sexual desire that cannot be satisfied in accordance with God's will and design. That's why lust is prohibited for both married and single people. Jesus said, "You have heard that it was said, 'Do not commit adultery.' But I tell you that anyone who looks at a woman lustfully has already committed adultery with her in his heart" (Matthew 5:27-28).

Just because there is no vaginal penetration doesn't mean you are not violating God's standard. Any behavior or thought that incites lust must be considered off-limits. Sexual arousal, like sex itself, is God-given. But sexual arousal that cannot be satisfied according to God's will and design is lust. It is prohibited. Therefore, any behavior—and that certainly includes oral sex, manual sex, what used to be called "heavy petting," and, dare I say it, even most kissing—should be avoided.

Even kissing? You might be thinking, *Alex, are you serious?* Yes, I am serious, but I'm not dogmatic on this point. Even the Bible says to "greet one another with a holy kiss." In many cultures kissing is a form of greeting. But that's not the kind of kissing I'm talking about. I'm talking about the kind of kissing that arouses you sexually.

More and more, young people are discovering the excitement and joy that comes, not just from remaining abstinent, but remaining chaste and pure. Don't get me wrong; too often I hear stories of increased teenage pregnancy, higher rates of sexually transmitted disease, and other tragic consequences of extramarital sexual activity. But I am also hearing stories of young people who have remained virgins until marriage. In fact, I regularly hear of young couples who kiss for the first time in front of the altar, with hundreds of family and friends gathered with them.

These couples know the truth of Jesus' words: "Blessed are the pure in heart, for they will see God" (Matthew 5:8). Seeing God in new, deep, and rich ways is what biblical marriage is all about.

Some Special Considerations

Homosexuality

Homosexuality is one of the hot button issues of our time. Much has been written about it by others, and much of what I could say is beyond the scope of this book, but let me make a couple of quick points.

First of all, it should be obvious that I believe homosexual behavior is a clear violation of God's law. Besides the specific injunctions against homosexuality in Scripture, homosexuality violates the principle of complementarity and the possibility of sex for procreation. Any way you look at it, homosexual behavior is out of bounds for Christians (Leviticus 20:13; Romans 1:26-27; 1 Corinthians 6:9; Jude 7).

There are those who say, however, that some men and women have a homosexual orientation. I'm going to say something here that is not universally accepted by evangelical Christians when I acknowledge that this may be true: Some people may indeed have a greater propensity for homosexuality than others. I have lived long enough to discover that there are more than 6 billion people on the planet, and we're all different. Scripture implies that some people are prone to a besetting sin (Hebrews 12:1). A besetting sin is one that is virtually irresistible to one person but which might be a complete nonissue for another. Everyone's besetting sin is different in some way, but they are all the same in this way: Just because a certain sin is hard to resist does not mean we get a pass on that sin. In God's eyes, sin is sin—whether large or small. All sin separates us from God.

I believe the same principle applies to homosexuality. Even if it is true that some people are genetically or physiologically predisposed to homosexuality (and there is no evidence that this is true), that does not excuse homosexual behavior. Homosexual behavior violates God's explicit commands, and it is counter to God's order for proper sexual behavior.

Masturbation

There is an old joke that goes something like this: "A new survey found that 90 percent of all men masturbate. The same survey found that 10 percent of all men are chronic liars."

Because there is a lot of truth in this old joke, it is no surprise that masturbation is the "third rail" when it comes to Christian discussions about sex. (On a subway or streetcar, the third rail is the rail that carries the electricity: Touch it and you die.) No one wants to touch the issue of masturbation because it is sure to elicit embarrassment and controversy.

Some Bible scholars believe that Scripture addresses the issue in Genesis 38. In that chapter, Onan's brother died. Onan was required by Jewish law to marry his brother's widow, Tamar. According to the law, any child that resulted from the marriage would not be considered Onan's son, but the son of Onan's brother. Onan dishonored the law, his brother, and Jewish law because he "spilled his semen on the ground" so that Tamar would not become pregnant. For this disrespect, Onan dies.

Though this story is not at all about masturbation, it has been interpreted to be a prohibition against masturbation. I find this story interesting and instructive—but not terribly convincing as a law against masturbation.

I believe that masturbation is wrong because it is impossible without lust. So even if the Bible does not prohibit masturbation, it does condemn lust.

Pornography revisited—learning from Ted Bundy

You will remember that in chapter 7 we talked about clear biblical injunctions against pornography. The Bible says it's wrong, and for the Christian that should be enough.

However, as I have said throughout this book, when the Bible gives us a "don't," there is always a good reason why. Indeed, one of my prayers for this book is that you will understand that the Bible and Christianity is not a list of do's and don'ts. The Bible is, more than anything, an adventure story and a love story. The adventure is nothing less than an account of the history of the entire world—the discovery of reality and truth. The love is the love that God has for you and me.

And because full participation in that adventure and in that love is so powerful, transformative, and healing, Satan will do anything to prevent that. One of his favorite strategies is to offer us counterfeits. Pornography is one such counterfeit, but it is a particularly destructive one. That destructive force was made clear by the life of Ted Bundy.

Bundy is not so well-known today, but there was a time when virtually every person in America knew his name. Until he was in college, Bundy was a more or less average guy. Indeed, you might even say he was above average. He was a Boy Scout, active in church, handsome, and well-spoken. He attended law school and was active in local politics. But none of these accomplishments were why people knew him. In the 1970s and 1980s, Bundy raped and murdered at least 30 young women, mostly on or near college campuses. He became known as one of the most notorious serial murderers in American history.

Just hours before Bundy was executed, in January 1989, radio host Dr. James Dobson interviewed him, and an important part of Bundy's story came out—how pornography had fueled his murderous desires.

Bundy told Dr. Dobson how he started looking at soft-core pornography at age 12—often finding the magazines in the garbage cans of his otherwise respectable neighbors. Soon, though, the soft-core porn could not provide the stimulation he had learned to crave, so he graduated to hard-core pornography, which he said became a "deadly habit" for him. Here are the words of a man full of remorse about his past, trying to warn others:

> My experience with pornography is that once you become
> addicted to it (and I look at this as a kind of addiction like
> other kinds of addiction), I would keep looking for more
> potent, more explicit, more graphic kinds of material. Like an
> addiction, you keep craving something that is harder, some-
> thing which gives you a greater sense of excitement. Until you
> reach a point where the pornography only goes so far, you
> reach that jumping off point where you begin to wonder if
> maybe actually doing it would give you that which is beyond
> just reading or looking at it.[5]

Bundy claimed to have made a profession of faith in Christ before his death. To celebrate Bundy's forgiveness before God is not to excuse his actions before man. I am simply pointing out the corrosive power that pornography can have on our minds and hearts. Pornography is not harmless fun. It is a damaging, corrosive force. Avoid it at all costs.

EVERYTEEN Megan—and You

If you are Megan (or Cameron), or someone who has already been sexually active or someone who is currently sexually active, it is easy to get discouraged by some of what was in this chapter: The impact of sexual activity is both profound and long-lasting. You might be thinking, *What's the point of trying? I've already gone past the point of no return.*

That's why I want to end this chapter by telling you that in God's mind there is no such place as the point of no return. God is in the business of forgiving and healing, no matter what the sin or how deep the wound.

You might be thinking, *But, Alex, I've done some pretty bad things.*

By the Book

Flee from sexual immorality. All other sins a man commits are outside his body, but he who sins sexually sins against his own body.

—*1 Corinthians 6:18*

■   ■   ■

To many, total abstinence is easier than perfect moderation.

—*Saint Augustine (354–430)*[6]

■   ■   ■

Whom have I in heaven but you? And earth has nothing I desire besides you.

—*Psalm 73:25*

Did you know that much of the Bible was written by just three men: Moses, Paul, and David? All three were murderers. God redeemed all three, and because of what God was able to do through them we're talking about them today. They literally changed history.

So nothing you have done is so bad that God can't forgive.

Or you might be saying, "But, Alex, I know God can forgive me, but I don't know how to get myself out of the mess I'm in."

All I can say is this: It's never too late to do the right thing. If you are in a sexual relationship, end it. No matter the current pain, end it. If your boyfriend or girlfriend dumps you because you're no longer having sex, then so be it. Your confession and forgiveness will lead to healing, and—no matter how painful the breakup is today—God can and will make you whole.

You have my word and God's Word on that.

Chapter 11

Spiritual Adventures

Have I not commanded you? Be **strong** and courageous. . . .

for the LORD your God will be with you wherever you go.

—Joshua 1:9

If someone told you, "I'm in great physical shape because I exercised every day for a year back in 1987," you'd know they were not only out of shape, but probably a bit crazy for even saying such a thing.

Or, to revisit an example I used back in chapter 5, imagine a young woman who asks, "I want to be a brain surgeon, and I've taken a biology class. Can I practice on your head?" No, you absolutely may not!

We know that anything worth doing—be it brain surgery, getting into physical shape, becoming an automobile mechanic, or mastering a musical instrument—will likely take years of focused attention and will require lifelong maintenance.

But somehow we think our spiritual lives operate differently from every other aspect of our lives. We think that if we've prayed a "sinner's prayer" to receive Jesus and been at least semiregular at youth group meetings, we are spiritually mature.

Now, I'm not knocking that, but it is not enough. Not nearly enough.

Confessing Failure

As I said in chapter 1, knowing that only two of six of my youth group "stars" went on to college and remained strong in their faith filled me with mixed emotion. Two are better than none, of course. But I grieved for the other four, and I wondered if I had somehow failed them, somehow let them down.

The truth is a bit complicated. With the experience I have today, I do think I could have done a better job preparing them for college and life beyond—and some of that wisdom, I hope you'll agree, is in this book.

But the rest of the truth is that I had actually beaten the odds a bit. Pollster George Barna tells us that only one in five high school seniors who say they are "born again" Christians and who go to evangelical churches are still exercising their faiths when they graduate from college. That's only 20 percent. Josh McDowell writes, "Between 70 and 94 percent of evangelical teens are leaving the traditional church after high school, and very few ever return."[1] So I guess my batting average wasn't so bad, after all.

But with the church's "batting average" being so bad, it is pretty pitiful to take any satisfaction in being only slightly better.

But if you've read this far, I'm going to assume that you are one of those who, by God's grace, has overcome the world. You've managed to hang on to faith in spite of some inept leadership. You want to go further and deeper with Jesus. For that I am both grateful and hopeful.

Approaching the Mysterious God

One of the most important things you need to learn about the Christian life is that it is a process, not an event. It's great to ask questions like "What Would Jesus Do?" But it is also important to remember that attempting to reduce God's will to a formula is one of the surest signs that you're on the wrong path. God is infinite. He will not fit into our boxes, no matter how large our boxes are. That means, among other things, that this side of eternity we will never really reach

By the Book

Better to love God and die unknown than to love the world
and be a hero;
better to be content with poverty than to die a slave to wealth;
better to have taken some risks and lost, than to have done
nothing and succeeded at it;
better to have lost some battles than to have retreated from
the war;
better to have failed when serving God, than to have succeeded when serving the devil.

What a tragedy to climb the ladder of success, only to discover
the ladder was leaning against the wrong wall.

—*Erwin Lutzer, pastor of The Moody Church*[2]

■ ■ ■

If you wish to possess finally all that is yours, give yourself
entirely to God.

—*Hadewijch, 13th century poet*[3]

■ ■ ■

I run in the path of your commands, for you have set my heart
free.

—*Psalm 119:32*

the goal of fully knowing God's perspective on things or fully knowing what "Jesus would do" in all the situations we face.

So, those of us who are pastors and teachers tend to reduce the infinite mystery of God down to the "Ten Steps to Spiritual Growth." Go into any Christian bookstore and you'll see what I mean. You can pick almost any topic—prayer, evangelism, leadership, personal finances, you name it—and you can find a book about that topic that reduces the subject to a few "simple" steps.

But God is bigger than any of these books. In fact, God is bigger than all of these books put together. Indeed, one of my greatest fears in writing *this* book is that it would be another of those that reduces the spiritual life to a few simple rules, when I know and you know that it is much more than that.

That's why I want to make sure you understand this: Your ultimate spiritual maturity is between you and God. The most I can hope to do is put you on the path, show you how to put one foot in front

Overheard in the Student Lounge

I think every Christian wonders, "What does God want me to do with my life?" Just obsessing about that can be kind of paralyzing. Think about a car sitting still, not moving. Don't sit like a parked car, praying over and over, "Lord, show me Your will for my life." Instead, put yourself in gear and start moving. The worst thing you can do is to never leave the garage! Do live morally, but take a stab at using some of the spiritual gifts God has given you. If you need to change direction down the road, God will be there with you.

—*Dawn L., Trinity Christian College, Illinois*

of the other, and tell you where you can go—to the Bible, to fellowship, and to prayer—to get sustenance for the journey.

Sustenance for the Journey

Get plugged in QUICKLY. When you arrive on campus, you will be assaulted with opportunities to fill your schedule. From clubs to service organizations, from sororities or fraternities to political groups, they will all compete for your time. But make getting involved in a Christian group a top priority. Most college campuses have at least a few great Christian groups. Some of the largest are Campus Crusade for Christ, InterVarsity Christian Fellowship, and the Navigators. (See Appendix II for their Web sites.) But many college campuses are also recruiting grounds for cults, so be wary. Here are a few suggestions for picking a campus ministry you can pour your life into. In return that ministry will help you find fellowship and spiritual growth.

Ask people you trust about the organizations on your campus. That might mean your current pastor or an older student from your church or community who is already active on campus.

Read doctrinal statements carefully. Check out the Web sites of the ministry. Be wary of ministries that will not fully disclose their core beliefs. A common strategy of cults is to share only innocent and vague information with a new "recruit," withholding dangerous doctrines and beliefs until an emotional connection is made. The Web sites should have doctrinal statements easily accessible and clearly understandable and will include the following:

- A clear statement that the Bible is the Word of God, the only authority for Christian living. (I prefer the word *inerrant*.)

- A clearly stated belief in the Triune God, or the Trinity. That means one God in three persons: Father, Son, and Holy Spirit.
- A belief in Jesus' literal and physical resurrection.
- The belief that salvation is through Christ alone, by faith alone.

Visit several groups before deciding which is right for you. Large campuses often have meetings of Christian groups several nights a week. Groups like Campus Crusade and InterVarsity often have large-group meetings once a week. These meetings are great for getting a feel for how the ministry operates on your campus.

Dig in deeply. But once you decide which group is right for you, make a commitment. One of the great values of campus ministries is that they also provide small-group interaction, where relationships can deepen and tough questions about the Christian faith can be explored. The larger groups also usually have a student leadership structure, with great training in Bible study, group facilitation, and even public speaking. Take advantage of these leadership development opportunities. Don't be a spectator; be an active participant.

Find a church home. I have spent much of my work career as a part of parachurch organizations such as Focus on the Family and the seminary of which I am not president. I believe that parachurch ministries such as these do much needed work on college campuses. If I didn't believe that, I wouldn't have recommended them to you. But I believe that the church is unique in "God's economy." I don't know exactly why God chose to do things this way, but He chooses to bless the church in a special way. So, on Sundays, get yourself to church. If you don't have a car, find a church close enough to campus to walk, or find a church with a bus or van ministry that serves your campus. I don't know of a church in the country that couldn't figure out a way to get you there if you told them that you really wanted to go!

But when looking for a church home, use the same kind of discretion and discernment that you use when examining a Christian ministry. Make sure any group you become involved with is classically orthodox and biblically sound.

Make spiritual disciplines a part of your schedule. I covered this pretty extensively in chapter 4, and again in chapter 8, so the only thing I will add here is a bit of motivation (and, perhaps, a bit of conviction) from Scripture:

> Do not be deceived: God cannot be mocked. A man reaps what he sows. The one who sows to please his sinful nature, from that nature will reap destruction; the one who sows to please the Spirit, from the Spirit will reap eternal life. Let us not become weary in doing good, for at the proper time we will reap a harvest if we do not give up. (Galatians 6:7-9)

Alex on His Soapbox

No good comes of a Christian in isolation. You are vulnerable to attack, to backsliding, to deception, and to discouragement. First Corinthians 12 gives us a good picture of the body of Christ at work: many members, one body. A hand or a foot severed from the body is not much use. Stay connected; be committed; find somewhere to serve.

If spiritual disciplines are a priority, you'll schedule them. If you don't schedule them, you're just kidding yourself if you say they're a priority. But you're not kidding God.

Pray alone, and pray with friends. The Bible says to "pray continually" (1 Thessalonians 5:17). So, obviously, prayer is vitally important to our Christian lives. This particular command means prayer should be a part of all aspects of life. Our hearts should be constantly in an attitude of prayer. I find that setting aside specific times of prayer is vital for my spiritual health, and setting aside time to pray with friends is a great way to hold yourself accountable for these times, and to develop unique relationships with your friends. I know of one young man who "fasted" from dating for a semester and spent every Friday night in prayer with a friend. If you have a Christian roommate, perhaps you could get together on a regular basis for prayer.

Find a mentor. In chapter 7, I introduced to you the idea of an accountability partner, someone who will meet with you regularly and ask you tough questions about your life to keep you honest with yourself and with God.

A good choice for an accountability partner is often someone who is a couple of years older than you, someone who can also serve as a mentor. In Scripture, Paul was a mentor to Timothy, and in a well-known passage, Paul tells Timothy of his responsibility to mentor others. "And the things you have heard me say in the presence of many witnesses entrust to reliable men who will also be qualified to teach others" (2 Timothy 2:2).

This passage outlines God's way of replicating spiritually mature disciples of Christ. In fact, it is not too much of a stretch to say that

A Word from the Faculty

Katelyn Steaffens, a junior at Biola University, is making a difference in the world. Her ministry revolves around Kid Works, an organization that serves families in the barrio of Orange County, California. From the seventh grade on, Katelyn has tutored groups of impoverished students thereby befriending and mentoring them as well.

Now as a junior in college with an intercultural studies major, Katelyn plans to be involved overseas in this type of ministry for years to come. She's been annually to Mexico, traveled in Guatemala on short-term missions, and co-led a Biola University missions team to Jamaica. This summer she'll be in South Africa working with AIDS victims. Next semester, she'll study and work in Egypt.

With her peers, Katelyn has served in a variety of ways. Katelyn has been elected to student body offices, various boards, and leadership positions on campus. In these capacities, her focus on service and her God-given gifts shine!

This sounds like a recommendation letter, and in a way it is. Students like Katelyn bring with them the warmth of Jesus Christ and His love. This is a student who makes a difference in lives internationally, in the inner city, in her peers. What a joy to see God mold young people who, for a time, grace my class, my office . . . my life!

—*Marla Campbell, Ph.D., professor of international studies,*
Biola University, California

every single Christian should be involved in a mentor relationship, either as the mentor or the "mentee," the one being mentored.

If you are a part of a parachurch ministry such as Campus Crusade, InterVarsity, or the Navigators, you can easily find a spiritual mentor. If you are willing, those organizations—and others like them—will put you in a small group under the leadership of an older student or staff member. Take advantage of these opportunities. Not only will you mature spiritually, but you will make friendships that will last a lifetime.

My two teens who succeeded discovered that Christianity was not a series of do's and don'ts. They learned that Christianity is a Great Adventure. Not only is it a relationship more fulfilling than any earthly relationship, but it opens your eyes to possibilities that no other view of the world can offer.

So if Christianity is all this, why do some still fall away?

As I have said, the way we teach Christianity is partly to blame. We want to *reduce* the truth of Christianity to something we can understand rather than *enlarge* our understanding so that we can fathom more of the truth of God. Indeed, it is that enlargement of ourselves—not for our glory, but for His—that is the great joy of Christianity.

And that is what the final chapter is all about.

Chapter 12

Life After College

This is what the LORD says:

"Let not the wise man boast of his wisdom

or the **strong** man boast of his strength

or the rich man boast of his riches,

but let him who boasts boast about this:

that he understands and knows me,

that I am the LORD, who exercises kindness,

justice and righteousness on earth,

for in these I delight."

—Jeremiah 9:23-24

What do you want to do when you grow up?

My guess is that when you were a child, adults by the dozens asked you this question, and you probably asked it of yourself and your friends. Perhaps in those days you even had an answer. A teacher. A doctor. A fireman. An astronaut. A professional baseball player. Perhaps all of the above!

When we're children, our decision-making process is simple. First, of all, we decide from the options we know about. Children might know about doctors and teachers—but not about accountants and financial analysts. We also make decisions based on our immediate wants and stimuli. In the 1960s, during the "race to the moon," millions of young kids wanted to be astronauts. Today, millions of kids want to be video game designers. Or, better yet, video game testers!

But as you get older, this question becomes more serious, and more difficult to answer. Being a doctor would be great, but do I want to go to school for another decade? I would love to be a writer or a musician, but can anyone really make a living at that—except for an elite few?

Reality begins to infringe on our dreams. There is a great temptation to settle for less than those dreams. To compromise. To sell out. To go with the first person or company who can "show me the money."

I believe that all of us have an inkling that dreams really can come true. In people with hard-core hedonist and materialist views, it is a nagging or gnawing feeling that they try to suppress with money or sex. In those who pay more attention to spiritual matters, it is a sense of purpose or destiny. No matter how hard we try, none of us can quite rid ourselves of the notion that God cares for us and has a great and wild plan for our lives.

Indeed, those who know me sometimes hear me talk of my "destiny meter." When I'm in the center of God's will for my life, I can almost feel the needle on my destiny meter pegging the red zone. You may have seen the great movie *Chariots of Fire*, about the runner Eric Liddell, who competed in the 1924 Olympics before giving his life as a missionary to China. In one of many moving scenes in that film, Eric tells his sister, "God made me for a purpose. But He also made me fast. When I run I feel His pleasure."[1]

We all want to know our purpose, to feel God's pleasure.

But how do we get there?

EVERYTEENS Erin and Joel

By Erin's junior year, she was thriving in leadership roles in a campus ministry. Nothing caused her more joy than teaching Scripture and seeing the light of understanding flicker and then burn brightly in the girls she was leading. Erin was not flashy or flamboyant, but by the time she was a senior, she had earned the respect of both the students and the staff ministers on the campus of her parachurch organization. But more important, Erin, like Eric Liddell, knew what it meant to feel God's pleasure.

■ ■ ■

When Joel first got to college, his roommate's devotion to the Church of Jesus Christ of Latter-day Saints caused him to examine the reliability of the Bible. He grappled with the question: *Is it possible that the Bible isn't true?*

But rather than rejecting his Christian heritage, he approached both Mormonism and strange philosophies—and the teachings of Christianity—with a desire to discover the truth. Joel discovered that the Bible can be trusted and that objections to Christianity can be answered with logical and solid answers. On the one hand he became convinced of God's love, power, and plan for his life. On the other, he found more evil in our society than he ever imagined was there. He wanted to do something about it.

God's View of Work

Because we have lost the idea that we are all called by God to fulfill a specific purpose in life, we—and I'm talking about Christians—have developed a flawed and destructive view of work.

Here's what the world thinks you should do with your life. (1) First, get a great education, an education that will empower you to become a successful and productive member of society. (2) When you're finished with your education, get a job that pays well, so you can buy a house and raise a family. (3) Begin saving early, because your kids will be going to college before you know it. (4) After that, you'll want to retire. And if you've planned well and worked hard, you don't have to wait until you're 65 to retire, but even if you do, don't worry.

Overheard in the Student Lounge

While working on my undergraduate degree in finance, I went to New York City for an internship and spent time on Wall Street passing out resumes, looking for a job. Quite literally, I was on the floor of the New York Stock Exchange, and I watched the people frantically looking at data on screens, yelling into their cell phones, pushing and shoving each other, and screaming as numbers changed. I knew that many of these people were successful, wealthy players in the financial world. I was working on my degree in finance in order to become one of them. But my time at the NYSE made me think twice. None of these people was happy, and it was every man for himself.

Later, while on the Staten Island ferry, I stared at a small stick floating by in the water. I knew that if I died and was floating dead in the Hudson River, no one would know or care. It wouldn't matter. There had to be more to life than the pursuit of a degree for the pursuit of money. About one month later, I became a Christian.

—Mike J., Maryland

There's still plenty of life ahead. In America, we're living to 75, 80, even longer. Just imagine: 10 years, 20 years, even more—all with no work and no worries. Is this a great life, or what?

Well, actually—no. It sounds like a great life, and—don't get me wrong—there are some good things in this description of the "good life." But almost every aspect of what I described runs against what the Bible teaches. Let's look at a few of them, one at a time.

God loves work. When God created the world, the Bible is very careful to call what He did "work" (Genesis 2:2) and at the end of each day God called His work "good." If God calls His own work good, and we are created in God's image, shouldn't the results of our work be good, too? I would suggest that most of us think of work as bad for one of two reasons. First, we've come to believe what the world is telling us, or—secondly—our work really is bad, at least for us. In other words, we are not doing the work God has called us to, but the work that we think we need in order to make money.

Education is for wisdom. We are told from earliest childhood that we need a good education so we can get a good job. There can be no doubt that Scripture strongly encourages education and study. In chapters 4 and 8 we covered this ground in some detail. And if you remember those chapters, you remember that the purpose of education is wisdom. Wisdom is more than just the accumulation of data and knowledge. Wisdom can be defined as having "God's mind" on things. It is developing what some have called a "moral imagination." In other words, it is developing the ability, as much as is humanly possible, to see the world as God sees it.

Developing the skills to earn a living is not a bad thing. Paul was a tentmaker and Jesus was a carpenter. But increasing your money-earning potential should never be the chief end of education.

The pursuit of wealth is condemned. In fact, Scripture tells us that the love of money is a root of all sorts of evil (1 Timothy 6:10). It is true that Scripture also indicates that wealth is sometimes a sign of God's blessing. Job was wealthy before his trials, and his wealth was restored tenfold afterward. Joseph of Arimathea is a somewhat shadowy figure in the Gospels. He is the man who paid for Jesus' burial, and was apparently both a follower of Jesus and a man of wealth and influence. But the "full counsel" of Scripture is that the accumulation of wealth is not a godly pursuit. Jesus said it is "easier for a camel to go through the eye of a needle than for a rich man to enter the kingdom of God" (Matthew 19:24). When Jesus instructs us how to pray, He says to pray for our "daily bread" (Matthew 6:11). This prayer is an echo of God's instruction to the Jewish people in the wilderness (Exodus 16:4), when He told them to collect only enough manna for that day, and not to accumulate extra. Again, hard work and thrift sometimes result in wealth, but working purely or mainly for the accumulation of wealth is clearly not the biblical standard.

Retirement is discouraged. It is hard to see how retirement is possible without the intentional accumulation of wealth. But even without that general principle to guide us, we have a specific passage in Scripture that deals with the issue:

> Someone in the crowd said to him, "Teacher, tell my brother to divide the inheritance with me."
>
> Jesus replied, "Man, who appointed me a judge or an arbiter between you?" Then he said to them, "Watch out! Be on your guard against all kinds of greed; a man's life does not consist in the abundance of his possessions."
>
> And he told them this parable: "The ground of a certain rich man produced a good crop. He thought to himself, 'What

shall I do? I have no place to store my crops.'

"Then he said, 'This is what I'll do. I will tear down my barns and build bigger ones, and there I will store all my grain and my goods. And I'll say to myself, "You have plenty of good things laid up for many years. Take life easy; eat, drink and be merry." '

"But God said to him, 'You fool! This very night your life will be demanded from you. Then who will get what you have prepared for yourself?'

"This is how it will be with anyone who stores up things for himself but is not rich toward God." (Luke 12:13-21)

Retirement is not in the Bible. The idea of retirement is a distinctly modern phenomenon. Most of our views about retirement are born of a materialistic view of the world and an incomplete or—in some cases—false view of Scripture.

Now, I know you're thinking to yourself, "But, Alex, I don't care about retirement. I haven't even had my first real job yet. What does all of this have to do with me?" Great question. But one of the "big ideas" of this book is that you should begin things with the end in mind. And if your goal in life is to work hard, make a lot of money, and retire young, then you'd better start now.

Alex on His Soapbox

A friend told me that when he turned 65, he decided to "retire." He set his wheels in motion in a new direction to serve God. View your entire life as an opportunity to serve God, not yourself.

But if your goal is to discern God's calling on your life, pursue that calling passionately and joyfully, and leave a spiritual legacy that will have eternal value. With that goal, then the path you start out on will be very different. Much of what you have learned about money, work, and your purpose in life could well be wrong and may have to be un-learned! I want you to know that wholeheartedly pursuing God's purpose for your life, and not career and money, is not easy to maintain over the course of the years.

But it is a path of great joy. And here are a few tips about how to do it.

Discovering God's Calling on Your Life

Does God really have a specific and personal calling on my life? Does God really care about me?

The Bible answers this question with a resounding and repeated yes. "For I know the plans I have for you, declares the LORD, plans to prosper you and not to harm you, plans to give you hope and a future" (Jeremiah 29:11). Jesus clearly knew His purpose in life. "I must preach the good news of the kingdom of God to the other towns also, because that is why I was sent" (Luke 4:43).

It is also true that historically the church has understood that God has a calling for each of us, and God has uniquely gifted each of us to fulfill that calling. "Now to each one the manifestation of the Spirit is given for the common good" (1 Corinthians 12:7). From there, Paul goes on to explain the various gifts of the Spirit. And he says that each of us, as we are gifted, is to fulfill a specific place within the body of Christ. Paul tells us to encourage each other in the exercise of our gifts and the fulfillment of our calling in the body of Christ. There are no "lesser" callings. "The eye cannot say to the hand, 'I don't need you!' And the head cannot say to the feet, 'I don't need you!' On the contrary, those parts of the body that seem to be weaker are indispensable" (1 Corinthians 12: 21-22).

I share those verses with you to make this point: God does have a purpose for your life, and it has very little to do with how much money you will make! It is about fulfilling your special calling and using to the fullest the gifts He has given you.

Having a Goal Is Not a Calling

I have a goal of writing this book, but I don't really believe that my calling is as a writer. I am a teacher and an evangelist. Those are my

By the Book

Avoiding danger is no safer in the long run than outright exposure. . . . Life is either a daring adventure, or nothing.

—*Helen Keller, deaf and blind American, author and activist (1880–1968)[2]*

■ ■ ■

I am not bound to succeed, I am bound to live by the light that I have.

—*Abraham Lincoln, 16th U.S. president (1809–1865)[3]*

■ ■ ■

Trust in the LORD with all your heart and lean not on your own understanding; in all your ways acknowledge him, and he will make your paths straight.

—*Proverbs 3:5-6*

gifts and my calling. Fortunately, being a teacher and an evangelist gives me skill at using words, and there are those around me—editors and proofreaders—whose gifts and calling complement my own.

The Terry Fox story

In the 1970s, a young man named Terry Fox had a goal to run track in college. But then something happened, which some might call tragic. Terry Fox was diagnosed with bone cancer. One of his legs was amputated six inches above the knee. Some might have cried out, "Why did God allow this to happen?" But if Terry Fox had those thoughts, he quickly put them behind him. As he was recovering from his surgery, he found his purpose in life. He saw the others in the cancer ward with him and resolved that his life purpose would be to eradicate cancer.

In order to help do that, he would run—on one good leg and one prosthetic leg—the length of his native Canada. His financial goal was to raise $1 million for cancer research. He called his plan the "Marathon of Hope."

Terry started his run in St. John's, Newfoundland, on April 12, 1980. Only a few people showed up to see him off, and the early parts of the trip were plagued with trouble. Terry had to run 26 miles a day, and then speak in local schools, churches, and civic clubs to raise money as he went. In sparsely populated and economically depressed Newfoundland, the going was tough. Terry had hoped to raise money for charity, but he was barely raising enough money to keep himself on the road.

But enthusiasm grew, media coverage followed, and by the time Terry ran into cities such as Quebec and Toronto, crowds into the thousands came to greet him.

Finishing the race, however, was not to be. On September 1,

A Word from the Faculty

I studied social science in college, and I enjoyed it. I was not a believer, or even seeking spiritually. I learned about the problems of the world and was taught that education and social programs were the solution. When a young woman from a cult sat next to me on a bus and began proselytizing me, I saw her zeal for her religion. I realized for the first time the great void in my life spiritually. I also recognized how vulnerable I was to that void being filled by something false. I began seeking.

When I returned to my hometown to attend graduate school, I began to hear the truth regularly at a local church. Although I was learning more social science, most of which was based on secular humanism, I received the encouragement and direction I needed at my church. There, where the pastor was both learned (having multiple degrees in theology and divinity) and strong in his faith, I learned that knowledge of the Word and exercising one's faith are not inherently antagonistic to academic knowledge and scholarly achievement; however, ideas, information, and scientific theories can be and should be evaluated in light of God's truth. Although the task of sorting out what was true seemed daunting to me then, I learned that with godly encouragement and support, along with prayer and Bible study, I could begin that journey. What is more, I have learned that the process is lifelong, fun, and rewarding, both intellectually and spiritually.

—*Lisa A. Seropian, Psy.D.,*
University of North Carolina, Charlotte

1980, Terry was feeling bad and suspended his run to seek medical attention. Doctors said the cancer had spread to his lungs, and the entire nation of Canada was stunned and saddened when Terry Fox died on June 28, 1981, at age 22.

It would be easy to say that Terry Fox failed. When he came off the road, he had not finished his goal of running across Canada, and he had not even raised the $1 million that he had hoped to give toward cancer research. Terry's original purpose, to cure cancer, mocked him as it was cancer itself that struck him down.

But that is not the end of the story. The courage of Terry Fox, the story of his run, and the grace and determination he showed in the last days of his life moved the world. To date, more than $400 million has been raised worldwide for cancer research in Terry's name through the annual Terry Fox Run, held across Canada and around the world. Cancer is not yet cured, but many think a cure will be found. Those in the know about such matters also say that the research funded by the Terry Fox Foundation will have played a key role.

Goals are good, but having a purpose and a vision for your life transcends goals. It would have been easy for Terry and his family to be angry and bitter because of the circumstances they faced. But it was these very challenges that gave Terry his life purpose and gave him a chance to serve millions, even after his death.

How Does God Show Us His Work for Us?

There is no simple formula for discovering God's calling on your life. In fact, now that we're approaching the end of this book, I hope you're beginning to discover that there is no easy formula for spiritual living.

But there are a few guidelines that might help you discover God's calling on your life.

He shows us affirmatively. If we are paying attention, we will discover that God is actively showing us His plan. We've already looked at a number of verses that say that explicitly, so I won't belabor the point here except to add this: Pay attention to the "still, small voice" within you.

He shows us as we ask in prayer. Jeremiah heard a specific instruction from the Lord: "Call to me and I will answer you and tell you great and unsearchable things you do not know" (Jeremiah 33:3). Though this verse applied to a particular place and time, I believe that it also applies to us today.

He shows us in His Word. If we study God's Word diligently, that understanding will give us an understanding of the path we should be on. Psalm 119:104 tells us, "I gain understanding from your precepts; therefore I hate every wrong path." When we study God's word, we have access to a supernatural wisdom and discernment regarding the path we should take.

He restrains us. There is a fascinating passage in Scripture, when David says of God, "You hem me in—behind and before; you have laid your hand upon me" (Psalm 139:5). Terry Fox wanted to run track in college. Cancer prevented that. Then he wanted to run across Canada. Cancer prevented that, too. But what God wanted was for the world to see Terry's grace and courage. Sometimes God withholds what we want so we can want what God wants to give us.

He shows us as we do it. In chapter 9, when we discussed ethics, you may remember that I said Christian ethics means not just knowing the right thing, but doing the right thing. So it is with God's purpose in our lives. When God shows us a direction, He expects us to obediently follow. We are looking for a storehouse of food, but God gives us manna for the day. We want a road map, but God gives us the next step. As Paul tells the Ephesians, even if you don't know the entire path before you, take the steps you do know to take: "Live a life worthy of the calling you have received" (Ephesians 4:1).

Our First Calling: To Be a Disciple

One of the most fascinating stories in the Bible is the story from Mark 5, when Jesus heals the man who was possessed by demons. The man wants to follow Jesus, but Jesus does a remarkable thing: He tells the man to return home. Can you imagine actually wanting to follow Jesus and being told by Jesus Himself that you can't? And it wasn't that Jesus didn't love the man. Jesus had traveled far from home for the very purpose of rescuing this man from the demons.

But for that man, this was the cost of discipleship; He had to sacrifice being in the physical presence of Jesus so that he could do the will of Jesus.

God has a calling for your life. I don't know what it is, but I do know that it is a great and mighty calling. It will require sacrifice and perseverance. It might not be what you originally think it should be, but God will not leave you hanging. He will show you the way.

It is my prayer that this book will help you follow that way and live that calling so that you will have a rich and powerful impact for the kingdom of God.

EVERYTEENS Epilogue

Here are the EVERYTEENS seven years later. But the real question is this: What do you want to be doing seven years after you graduate?

EVERYTEEN Adam dropped out of school to work in a lumberyard where he finally learned discipline. His partying was curtailed because he had to start work at 5 A.M. He earned his A.A. degree in business. He's still hoping to get a bachelor's degree, but it will have to wait until he can save the money. He is attending church regularly because he still lives with his parents, who make sure he goes every Sunday.

EVERYTEEN Cameron earned a Ph.D. in psychology and now specializes in counseling people struggling with gender identity issues. He ran for mayor in a small town in northern California to get rid of the conservative incumbent, and lost; however, he plans to run again. He'll eventually win; after all, he's a smart guy.

EVERYTEEN David is a city auditor in New England. He still cheats.

EVERYTEEN Erin joined the staff of Campus Crusade for Christ. She takes ministry trips all over the world. During her senior year in college, Erin's mother became a Christian, and her father is open to attending church.

EVERYTEEN Joel got through college, got married, and has twin girls. His wife is supportive of his going to seminary part-time so that he can become a pastor.

EVERYTEEN Megan has two kids, a workaholic husband (John) who cares more about the car than God, and a thousand regrets on what might have been.

Stand Strong Answers 20 Questions

Questions About God

Q1. Can anyone really be sure that God exists?

From the first verse in Genesis and throughout the Bible, the presence of God is deemed a given. The Bible never tries to defend or explain His existence. In fact, Scripture calls anyone who doesn't believe in God a fool (Psalm 14:1). Ouch!

Some people, however, do not accept God's presence as an unquestionable fact and yet are still seeking Him earnestly. There is a difference between foolishness and honest doubt. When addressing concerns about God's existence, begin by offering loving reassurance that belief in God is reasonable and logical.

God is knowable, because He wants to be. He has shown the world that He exists through creation, conscience, Scripture, and the Savior. (Just remember C.C.S.S.). Creation cries out for a Creator (Acts 17:16-34). The moral law written on our conscience cries out that there is a Lawgiver (Romans 2:11-16). The content of Scripture and the life of our Savior can be explained only in terms of divine origin (see questions 6 and 10 for further explanations). In other words, the evidence for God is there. While God invites us to come to Him in faith, belief is a completely rational position to embrace.

The issue is logical but also transcends mere intellectualism; humans are offered a life-changing relationship with God Himself. That's where God has revealed Himself most completely of all—in the person of His Son, Jesus Christ.

Q2. Why does God allow evil and suffering in the world?

God does not directly cause evil actions or suffering. God may *allow* such things to occur, but Christians do not blame Him for *causing* them.

Yes, God has allowed pain to exist in this world, and yet because He is all-loving, He must have good and just—morally sufficient—reasons for allowing such suffering. God has a plan and is working toward some greater good. Given a particular instance of pain (a teen died in a car crash; arsonists burned down the inner-city hospital) we cannot always discern that any good will result. We don't know everything that God does, but we can trust that a great good will result.

If we accept that God is all-powerful (divine omnipotence), that God has all knowledge (divine omniscience), and that God is all good (omni-benevolence), we may be justified in trusting that God has sufficient reason for the pain He allows His creation to endure.

God is no stranger to pain; evil grieves Him, too (Genesis 6:5-7; Isaiah 63:10). Before He went to the cross, Jesus was sorrowful "to the point of death" (Mark 14:34). Jesus endured incredible suffering on the cross for our good. God's mercy, love, and comfort are available to those who ask for His help (Psalm 23:4; 119:50; Matthew 5:4; 2 Corinthians 1:3-7).

Q3. Does the Bible present two Gods—a judgmental Old Testament God and a loving New Testament God?

Throughout the Bible it is clear that there is one God: "Hear, O Israel: The LORD our God, the LORD is one" (Deuteronomy 6:4). Jesus affirmed this (Mark 12:29), as did Paul (1 Corinthians 8:4; 1 Timothy 2:5).

The Bible does not show a judgmental God in the Old Testament and an all-loving God in the New Testament. Yes, in the Old Testament you read about God wiping out entire cities such as Sodom and Gomorrah. But you also read about His unfailing love and mercy (Exodus 20:6; Deuteronomy 7:9; Jeremiah 31:3; Psalm 25:6; 100:5). In the New, Jesus heals the sick, but He also makes 10 references to hell and uses some fierce language when talking about sinners (see Matthew 23:33 for one example). Revelation 20:15 shows a New Testament God who will cast people into a lake of fire.

The attributes of God are presented exactly the same in both the Old and New Testaments: He has always been and always will be concerned about both love and justice.

Q4. Could God create a rock so big that even He couldn't lift it?

Ever heard the saying, "If I had a nickel for every time someone had asked me this, I'd be rich"? Well, insert that phrase here! Some people actually think that this little logic puzzle somehow puts God in checkmate. Let's unpack this loaded question.

The challenge inherent is whether there's something God cannot do. If we determine there is something God cannot accomplish, then we can prove He is limited and less than almighty. It's actually a pseudoquestion much like this one: Can God make a square circle? The question makes no sense because it pits two incompatible definitions against each another.

The question also reveals false ideas about the biblical concept of omnipotence. Omnipotence does not mean God has the power to do *anything*. Being all-powerful means that God can do anything consistent with His character and who He is. God cannot do something that is contrary to His nature. He cannot lie or sin.

It is a logical impossibility—a nonsensical thing—to fault God for not being able to make a rock so big that He couldn't lift it. We may as well demand that God make two men, each one taller than the other.

On the Bible and Christianity

Q5. What does it mean to be a Christian?

The biblical definition is clear: A Christian is a follower of Christ.

Jesus said that to be saved a person must be "born again," or "born from above" (John 3). To become a Christian, you must admit that you are separated from God by sin. Jesus said that each person must repent (turn away) from his or her sin (Luke 13:3). Salvation is a free gift, undeserved, not something that can be earned.

Believing in Jesus means that we accept *who* He is (the Son of God, see question 10) and *what* He did (died for our sins and rose again). But a true Christian has accepted the responsibility to be committed to follow Jesus Christ for life.

Christianity is both an *event* and a *process*. Salvation is a one-time *experience*; the spiritual growth that will follow is a lifelong *adventure*. A Christian will desire to know God more and more, read His Word, and endeavor to obey Him fully in all areas of life.

Q6. How do we know that the Bible was given by God?

The Bible was written by at least 40 authors over a 1,500-year period, and yet the 66 books carry a unified message of God's love and salvation. Volumes have been written about the Bible's unique characteristics, including its apparent indestructibility and its historical, scientific, and prophetic truths.

The trustworthiness of Scripture is clearly addressed internally. The Bible states, "Your word, O LORD, is eternal" (Psalm 119:89), "Every word of God is flawless" (Proverbs 30:5), and "The Scripture cannot be broken" (John 10:35). But to quit there would leave us staking eternity on circular reasoning. Truth seekers want more evidence than "It's true because it says it's true." Fortunately, other facts testify on behalf of the Bible's accuracy.

By historical standards, the Old Testament is trustworthy. As Jewish scribes made copies of those Scriptures, they counted the letters on each page—forward and backward, on the master copy and the new edition—to ensure that nothing was added or omitted. Though the Old Testament comes to us through a comparatively fewer number of known manuscripts than the New Testament, the books have been meticulously preserved. In fact, a copy of Isaiah found among the Dead Sea Scrolls and dated to about 200 B.C. was virtually identical to the next oldest copy we have, which is dated to around A.D. 900. That's 1,100 years of faithful transmission on this book alone.

Confidence in the New Testament lies in the amazing number of copies discovered. In addition to the books themselves, more than 86,000 quotations of individual verses by early Christians have been found. They date from within 150 to 200 years of the time of Christ and dramatically illustrate the familiarity that ancient Christians had with the New Testament Scriptures.

Comparing the New Testament with secular writings from the ancient world, the Bible's closest peer could be Homer's *The Iliad,* a manuscript existing in more than 600 copies. Homer beats Aristotle but still can't hold a candle to the Bible. The number of ancient texts containing all or part of the New Testament number around 30,000.

The book of Acts cites at least 84 historical facts verified by later research and archaeology. Luke's accuracy regarding details, names, and places has been acknowledged by numerous historians. This same author also mentions 35 miracles in Acts. Why would Luke have been meticulously accurate in his history and misleading when talking of other things? Indeed, Scripture is dependable for its statements about history and destiny, the physical world, and spiritual realities.

Our view of Scripture should be in harmony with that of Jesus. Christ affirmed the Old Testament (Matthew 5:18; Luke 24:44) and made provision for the soon-to-come New Testament (John 14:26). These facts, when taken together, point out that an all-powerful God certainly could create such a document, but is it reasonable to accept that He did? The external evidence, the Bible itself, and the risen Jesus all say yes.

Q7. Were miracle stories crafted after Jesus died and then included in Matthew, Mark, Luke, and John just to make Jesus look like a wonder-worker or Jewish messianic figure?

First, let's examine the wonder-worker angle. Suppose the early believers were *trying* to make Jesus out to look like a wonder-worker. Only two Old Testament prophets were also big-time miracle workers: Elijah and Moses. If they were trying to force a comparison with those two, they would have accentuated the similarities. But the opposite is true: Jesus disassociated Himself from the prophets.

Jesus denied He was Elijah (Matthew 16:13-17) and in fact said John the Baptist had that role (Matthew 11:14). The only miracle in common between Moses and Jesus is feeding many with bread, and it's a stretch to compare the manna that God provided for the Israelites with Jesus' feeding of the multitudes (Exodus 16; John 6:1-14). Additionally, Jesus used this miracle to show that He is the bread of life, which was not Moses' purpose. In John 3:14-15 the Bible says Jesus likened Himself to the golden snake that Moses raised (Numbers 21:9), but these links aren't sufficient to merit an identification between Moses' wonders and Jesus'. Jesus is not, wasn't trying to be, didn't want to be Moses II.

Now let's look at the charge that Jesus' followers wanted Him to appear as a messianic figure. The Jews of that time expected their Messiah to free Israel from Roman control, but Jesus, instead of conquering the Romans, died by Roman execution. Jesus' primary miracle was His resurrection from the dead, which wasn't expected by Jews of Jesus' time even in their wildest dreams.

The Gospels were written within the lifetime of eyewitnesses of Jesus' life (1 Corinthians 15:6). It would have been easy to refute a made-up story.

Q8. Don't the resurrection accounts hopelessly contradict one another?

No. In fact, if the resurrection accounts presented in the four Gospels were in seamless agreement, skeptics would probably accuse the early church of having engaged in some sort of conspiracy. If the police hear the exact same story from witnesses, for example, they become suspicious. It means the witnesses probably got together and made it up. The unique attributes of each gospel account actually contribute to the overall authenticity of testimony for Jesus' resurrection.

On the surface there may seem to be *apparent* discrepancies, but there are no *actual* contradictions. The truth is that no single account of the resurrection completely exhausts the event. Just as different eyewitnesses to an accident will give varying testimonies, all of which are true, the "reporters" of the resurrection chose to include the details that were important to them. There is a basic order given in all of the resurrection accounts that when studied removes the apparent contradictions.

Here is that basic order of Christ's appearances:

Mary Magdalene	John 20:11-14
To "the other women"	Matthew 28:9-10
Peter	Luke 24:34
Two disciples	Luke 24:13-32
Ten apostles	Luke 24:33-49
Thomas and "the other apostles"	John 20:26-30
Seven apostles	John 21
To all the apostles	Matthew 28:16-20
To the 11 disciples	Acts 1:4-9
To 500 brethren at once	1 Corinthians 15:6
James	1 Corinthians 15:7
Paul	1 Corinthians 15:7

Q9. My professor said that most of Christianity is based on the ideas of Paul rather than on Jesus' teachings. How should I respond to this?

Many scholars embrace Jesus' Sermon on the Mount (Matthew 5–7), which includes ideas such as "love your neighbor" and "feed the poor." The same scholars, however, want to throw out Paul's teachings because he comments about controversial issues that are not included in the Gospels such as homosexuality and women as pastors.

Before we discuss Paul's teaching in particular, we need to discuss whether the words of Christ as recorded in the Gospels are more important than other writings in the Bible. Let's think of the Bible in three categories:

1. The Old Testament
2. The words of Jesus (the "red letters")
3. The rest of the New Testament other than Jesus' words

The Old Testament writings were valid to Jesus. He did not come to abolish the teachings of the Old Testament, but to fulfill them

(Matthew 5:17). Additionally Jesus affirmed the Old Testament by quoting it many times and taught that the authority of Scripture was timeless (Matthew 24:35; John 10:35). Per Jesus, the Old Testament teachings are truth even though God used men to write the words.

The words of Jesus, the second category of text we're looking at, are revered to the extent that many Bibles use a special color (usually red) to print them. Jesus' words are usually the first evidence presented when scholars discuss theological issues. Most Christians take the words of Christ seriously and consider them the words of God Himself.

The defense for the third category, which includes Paul's letters and sermons, starts with the words of Jesus in John 14:26: "The Holy Spirit, whom the Father will send in my name, will teach you all things and will remind you of everything I have said to you." Jesus in effect knew the Holy Spirit would come and continue to teach the disciples. Paul's letters and the rest of the New Testament are part of the "all things" and were given to us by the Holy Spirit, so they are also in effect the words of God even though men wrote them down.

In summary, the Old Testament, the words of Jesus, and the rest of the New Testament are all equally valid sources of truth and do not contradict each other. (For more on why we can trust the Bible, see question 8.)

Let's get back to the question of whether or not the apostle Paul invented Christianity. Paul started out his career as a passionate persecutor of the church; he even had Christians stoned to death. Then Paul became a believer about A.D. 35. The book of Acts, which was written by Luke, records Paul's salvation experience in chapters 9, 22, and 26. In his own writings, Paul also explains his conversion to faith (1 Corinthians 9:1; 15:3-8; Galatians 1:11-18). From about A.D. 48 until his death around A.D. 68, Paul wrote at least 13 of the New Testament's books.

The fact that Paul had originally opposed and persecuted the church proves that he could not have invented Christianity. If Paul persecuted Christians, there had to be Christians who converted before he did, otherwise there would have been no one to persecute.

Additionally, in 1 Corinthians 15:3-8, Paul's used the words "received" and "passed on" in reference to the good news. In relating the facts about Jesus' death and resurrection, Paul is saying that he heard the story from someone else, so he couldn't have started it.

Before Paul became a Christian, Peter and his crew were doing their best to spread the story. Look at Peter's sermon at Pentecost, found in Acts 2:14-40. Peter presents the core facts of the gospel, including Jesus' divinity, death, and resurrection. Peter preaches the same truths again in Acts 3:12-18. In Acts 5:29-33, Peter addressed Jewish leaders, and again gives the key facts of the Christian message. In Acts 5:42, we read that "day after day, in the temple courts and from house to house, they never stopped teaching and proclaiming the good news that Jesus is the Christ."

You can tell your professor with confidence that the key teachings of the gospel were well established before Paul became a Christian. Paul taught these things, expounded on these things, and was used by God to write much of the New Testament. But the core of the gospel was being widely spread even before Paul was a believer. In 1 Corinthians 15:8, even Paul admits that he was late getting to the party!

Q10. Did Jesus really claim to be God, or did His followers just say that about Him?

I often say that Jesus Christ was either the world's greatest truth-teller or history's greatest blasphemer. In a number of verses (Matthew 26:64-65; Mark 14:62, 64; Luke 22:66-71) Jesus affirmed that He is Deity, that is, God.

Additionally, Jesus said that people will die spiritually if they do not entrust their souls to Him (John 8:24). If Jesus spoke the truth, was the real deal, and did what He did in order to save the souls of humanity, then He should be praised as having been the greatest truth-teller.

We have no reason to believe that Jesus was mistaken about His identity, nor was He intentionally trying to mislead His followers. His incredible claims and miraculous life were coupled with an unparalleled type of confirming proof: He rose from the grave. Clearly, we have legitimate reason to accept that Jesus is the Son of God.

Jesus did other things to affirm He was the true God:

Matthew 23:34—Jesus was the One who sent prophets to Israel

Mark 2:10—Jesus is able to forgive sin

Mark 2:28—Jesus is Lord over the Jewish Sabbath

Luke 4:21 and John 5:39—Jesus refers to Himself as the fulfillment of Scripture

John 8:24—To reject Jesus is to die in sin

John 8:36—Jesus can truly set people free

John 8:42—Jesus came from God

John 8:58—Jesus is eternal

John 10:30—Jesus has the same nature as God the Father

John 13:13—Jesus is Lord

John 14:6—Jesus is the only way to God

John 14:9—If you have seen Jesus, you have seen the Father

Jesus claimed attributes for Himself that are appropriate only to God. In essence, Jesus taught, "What you do with me will determine where you spend eternity." In light of the fact that Jesus' unique claims were accompanied by miraculous deeds and a sinless life, each person would do well to respond to the things He taught.

Q11. Why do Christians think that their beliefs are correct and everyone else's are false?

The number one thing that sets Christianity apart from other religions is that Christianity offers a relationship with a living, death-conquering Savior. In other words, our God is alive! Yes, knowledge of this makes us bold! Sorry about that!

When Christians claim the Bible's content has been preserved and remains unchanged through the centuries or that Jesus Christ was crucified 2,000 years ago during Passover and rose from the grave, it's much more than just personal opinion. Christianity alone is a belief system offering *objective* truth. Christianity does not ask people to give their lives for *human opinion*. Additionally, Christians are people who have experienced a *relationship* with the Person who said He was the personification of truth.

Christians (like adherents of other belief systems) think their teachings are true. But contradictory truth claims cannot both be correct at the same time. For instance, Christians say that Jesus was crucified, and Muslims say that Jesus was not crucified. It cannot be true that Jesus both *was* crucified and *was not* crucified. One system must be wrong.

Jesus said that no one could come to God but through Him (John 14:6). Was Jesus right about this, or was He wrong? He could not both *be* the Savior and also *not be* the Savior. Either He was or He wasn't. The point is that Christians do not insist that their beliefs are true out of pride or stubbornness.

The Christian faith is justifiable in light of the compelling evidence (rational and historical) that accompanies the claims. The Christian teachings and claims may be examined, tested, empirically investigated, and evaluated for their plausibility. In other words, Christianity is *objectively true*. No other belief system can claim this.

Q12. What happens to people who haven't heard about Jesus or the gospel?

The short answer is this: Apart from Jesus Christ, no one is saved, and because people sin, they will perish.

People recoil at this truth and feel it is unjust because many people have never heard the gospel. The Bible (a book shown to be trustworthy; see question 6) explains that every person is given truth about God. God's existence and nature are revealed through the created world (Romans 1). The duties of God's moral law are known to each of us through our conscience (Romans 2). We also carry within us the nagging realization that we have disobeyed God's laws, and we are aware that we have done wrong things. In short, people everywhere seem cognizant of their own *sin.*

Regarding the fate of lost souls, Christian thinker and mathematician Blaise Pascal reasoned in the following way: The Bible promises that all who seek God will find Him. But not all find God. Therefore, *despite appearances,* not all sought God.

Each person also has the chance to respond to the amount of truth that God has given him or her. Because we know that God is all-loving and all-powerful, we may be confident that He will do everything possible to give each person an opportunity to respond to truth. We may be certain the final judgment will be *fair.* More than that, it will be appropriate and merciful, because that is God's nature.

P.S. If you're worried about people going to hell, there's a solution: Share the gospel!

On Social Issues and Cults

Q13. Why do Christians pick on gays? Shouldn't we love them?

Homosexuals are people created and loved by God. So Christians must show love to gays. But the Bible—plus natural law—tells us that homosexual acts are sinful and unnatural (1 Corinthians 6:9; Romans 1:24-27). Just as adulterous acts are sinful, homosexual acts are classified as sinful.

If Christians truly love a person, they will act in a way that is best for that person. That might include telling a homosexual that he or she is behaving in a way that displeases God. This may seem like "picking on" someone. But if homosexual acts are sinful, loving a gay person involves helping that person to discontinue his or her homosexual behavior.

When shown true love in a considerate manner, all people in bondage to sin will be discouraged from continuing. Jesus and Paul would have treated homosexuals with respect (John 8:3-11; 1 Corinthians 5:1-5). The mere fact that someone is sinning doesn't give a Christian an excuse to treat that person with contempt. But neither does the lack of tactfulness shown by Christians give a homosexual an excuse to persist in sinful practices.

Q14. What do I say to a Jehovah's Witness?

The Jehovah's Witnesses, an aggressively evangelistic group, are growing in numbers and teach a message radically different from that of orthodox Christianity. Discussing Bible verses with one of their members is most likely futile because the Jehovah's Witnesses use their own unique "translation" to prove their doctrines. They are taught that traditional Christian doctrine is the product of Satan, and when a Christian argues with the teachings of the Watchtower Society (the official name of the Jehovah's Witnesses organization), the argument is seen as a confirmation of this.

Because all Jehovah's Witnesses are taught that only the Watchtower Society's interpretation of the Bible is accurate, it's best to begin a discussion there. If you can discredit the reliability of the Watchtower Society on the basis of false prophecies and contradictions, you can discredit the specific Jehovah's Witnesses doctrines.

For instance, Jehovah's Witnesses have predicted Christ's return three times: 1917, 1918, and 1925. By 1931 they learned to quit fixing dates. In 1968 Jehovah's Witnesses admitted that specific past predictions of the end to the world had failed. They were guilty of false prophesy. Why? What was missing? Only this: Evidence of truth and that God is guiding them.

Christians know from Deuteronomy 18:21-22 that "if what a prophet proclaims in the name of the LORD does not take place or come true, that is a message the LORD has not spoken." Jehovah's Witnesses doctrine does not pass the test.

Q15. Why are Christians so hypocritical? They're no better than anyone else.

A born-again Christian is a *forgiven* hypocrite—a saved hypocrite—but a hypocrite nonetheless. So to the person who says, "Christians are at times hypocritical," I say, "Yes. And so are non-Christians."

The Bible says that all persons are sinners. We are sinners by birth (Psalm 51:5). We are also sinners by choice, because we know what's right, yet we often do what's wrong (James 4:17). In the day that we all stand before God, the Bible says each person's conscience will either *accuse* or *excuse* him (Romans 2:15-16). The ultimate questions are not, "Have I lived a perfect life? Was I ever hypocritical?" They are, "What did I do with Jesus? What was my response to God's offer of forgiveness through His Son?"

Because everyone at times acts as a hypocrite, this objection is simply an attack against hypocrisy. It says nothing about the truth or falsity of Christian truth claims—except to reinforce the idea that everyone has sinned. The unfortunate fact that Christians are sometimes hypocritical says nothing about whether or not God exists, weather the Bible is true, or if Jesus was authentic. The Christian faith does not rest upon the validity of its messengers; it rests upon the validity of its message.

Q16. What is the best way to share the gospel with a Mormon?

Share the gospel with a member of the Church of Jesus Christ of Latter-day Saints by demonstrating the essential differences between Christian and Mormon doctrine. This will allow you to present the essentials of the gospel, and it allows the Mormon to see that Christianity and Mormonism do not agree when it comes to core biblical truths. Here are some areas where the essentials are in conflict:

Christianity	Mormonism
God: One God, eternal and unchanging, Spirit with no physical body.	**God:** Many gods, changeable, was once a mortal man, physical body.
Christ: Eternally God, uncreated and Creator of all things, unique Son of God.	**Christ:** Not eternally God, procreated as the first spirit-child, spirit brother of Lucifer (Satan),
Trinity: Father, Son, and Holy Spirit are one in nature and three in persons, offers eternal life as a free gift.	**Trinity:** Three distinct beings or gods, offers a chance to earn eternal life.
Holy Spirit: The Holy Spirit is God.	**Holy Spirit:** The Holy Spirit is *a* god.
Salvation: Atonement of Christ and faith alone, grace alone, salvation is given based on Christ's perfection, not the individual's.	**Salvation:** Atonement of the Mormon Jesus requires grace *and* works, salvation is revealed but cannot be attained unless each person becomes perfect by his personal works of righteousness.
Goal: To live eternally with God.	**Goal:** To live eternally as a god.

End the conversation by discussing Jude 1:3 and the fact that "the faith that was once for all entrusted to the saints" and therefore the original gospel is the correct one.

The Bible clearly warns us against embracing a false gospel. Paul wrote in Galatians 1:8, "But even if we or an angel from heaven should preach a gospel other than the one we preached to you, let him be eternally condemned!" He also said, "Satan himself masquerades as an angel of light. It is not surprising, then, if his servants masquerade as servants of righteousness. Their end will be what their actions deserve" (2 Corinthians 11:14-15).

Q17. How can I share Christ with this Muslim guy in my dorm?

When sharing Christ with a Muslim, I quickly begin to discuss our specific religious teachings. I do not gloss over or ignore the great differences in our belief system. For example, Islamic teachings do not mesh with the fundamental Christian beliefs in the Trinity and Jesus' divinity.

Muslims have a high level of respect for the Bible, though they will need to be shown that the New Testament is accurate and can be trusted in what it says about Jesus. They say that the Bible has been corrupted and changed. Ask the Muslim, "What are the changes in the Bible, and when were they introduced?" He will not be able to answer, because the text has been meticulously preserved (see question 6).

Point out that the Prophet of Christianity (Jesus) is unique in that He was a loving and sinless Savior (in suras 40:55 and 48:1-2, the Qur'an teaches that Muhammad was a sinner). Muslims say that Christ *did not* die on the cross, so they need to be shown that Jesus was qualified to die sacrificially and capable of rising from the dead. Emphasize that Christians have an intimate, *personal* relationship with Jesus and have great joy in knowing that they are secure in Christ (see John 10:28-29).

Make a positive case *for* Christianity. Explain that Christians agree there is only one God (Deuteronomy 6:4; Isaiah 43:10-11). We who espouse the Trinity do not believe in three Gods. Gently remind Muslims that where one stands with God is the most important issue of life—more important than culture, family background, or social customs. Sharing Jesus with U.S. Muslims is a continual reminder of the uniqueness and power of the gospel message.

It is important to remain friendly and humble, and to avoid an air of superiority at all cost. The most important steps in evangelism among Muslims, however, are *pray, pray, pray!*

Q18. What really is "white magic," and is it okay for Christians?

Those who practice white magic believe that they are using supernatural powers for the good. Black magic is done for evil purposes. Many occultists, however, say there is no real distinction between the two types.

In the Bible we read that God condemns all forms of occult practices. In Deuteronomy 18:10-12, sorcery is condemned. Sorcery includes all forms of magic, white or black. We are warned that Satan tries to make his powers look good (2 Corinthians 11:12-14). God does not distinguish between white magic and black magic but forbids all forms of magic and sorcery. Other passages that address this include the following: Leviticus 19:26; 2 Kings 17:17; 21:6; Isaiah 47:9-12; Ezekiel 13:20; Acts 8:9; 13:8; 19:19; Galatians 5:20; and Revelation 21:8. God is the true source of power and life (Exodus 8:18-19; Daniel 1:20). He created the universe from nothing and resurrected Jesus from the dead. It is not only fraudulent to seek meaning and empowerment elsewhere, it is spiritually dangerous.

Q19. What is the discussion over "intelligent design" all about?

Intelligent design (sometimes called "design theory" or "ID") is a position regarding life's origins. To be clear, ID is *not* an argument for the Bible or for the gospel of Jesus Christ, specifically. Educator and author William Dembski said, "This is a very modest, minimalist position. It doesn't speculate about a creator or his intentions."[1] But ID is an admission of the obvious: The complexities of this world are best explained and understood in terms of intelligent causes, and the empirical evidence supports this conclusion.

In his book *No Free Lunch: Why Specified Complexity Cannot Be Purchased Without Intelligence,* Dembski observes, "The evidence for Darwinism was never any good—even in Darwin's day. But with advances in contemporary science, Darwinism becomes utterly unsupportable."[2] Living organisms are composed of functioning parts that work in well-ordered ways. The absence of even one part would render the entire creature or organ inoperable.

Wrap your mind around this: An individual cell, made up of 10 quadrillion atoms, is more complex than a giant factory. It possesses and manages more information than is contained in a full set of *Encyclopaedia Britannica.* Consider also that there are 34 trillion copies of your own DNA—an information "recipe" for you—encoded, arranged, and stored by means of four characters. Observing a cell's ability to collect, arrange, and collate data (all functions requiring intelligence), one scientist noted, "What remains overwhelmingly impressive is that a single cell can do more than our most powerful supercomputers."[3]

NASA astronomer John O'Keefe said, "If the Universe had not been made with the most exacting precision we could never have come into existence. It is my view that these circumstances indicate the Universe was created for man to live in."[4] Renowned Cambridge scientist Fred Hoyle famously compared the likelihood of even one biological molecule forming via chance to filling the entire solar system with blind men, each handling a Rubik's Cube, and all accidentally solving the puzzle at the same time. In other words, it's impossible—apart from intelligent intervention.[5]

By comparison, believing that life somehow evolved from the primordial slime is a huge leap of faith. In the *Annual Review of Ecology and Systematics,* N. A. Takahata stated, "We have no direct access to the processes of evolution, so objective reconstruction of the vanished past can be achieved only by creative imagination."[6] A paleontologist who searched in vain for transitional life forms told *U.S News & World Report,* "If we can't find the fossils, sometimes you have to think that they just weren't there."[7]

In recent court cases, inclusion of ID teaching in public schools has suffered temporary setbacks. But evangelicals need not be ashamed to voice their belief in God the Creator. Biology and earth-science students especially will be encouraged to know that increasing numbers of scholars, professors, and published scientists are voicing doubts about Darwinism and support for Intelligent Design.

Q20. What is apologetics?

Christian apologetics is the discipline that deals with a rational defense of Christianity. Our term *apologetics* comes from the Greek word *apologia,* which means, "to give a reason or defense." For the Christian, apologetics may include effectively explaining why we believe that God is real, the Bible is true, and Jesus is authentic.

First Peter 3:15 contains the admonition, "Always be prepared to give an answer to everyone who asks you to give the reason for the hope that you have." The same wording is found in Philippians 1:7 and 1:16, where Paul said that he is "appointed for the defense of the gospel" (NKJV). The principle is echoed in Jude 3, as believers are encouraged to earnestly "contend for the faith."

Categories of Christian apologetics include: (1) Textual apologetics—defending the authority and trustworthiness of Scripture and then presenting its content; (2) Evidential apologetics—presenting the many evidences in defense of the Christian faith; and (3) Philosophical apologetics—exposing the flawed reasoning behind many of the popular arguments against Christianity.

Ironically, many people today think they have legitimate reasons for rejecting Jesus Christ and that God does *not* have justifiable claim on their lives. The Bible says that those who suppressed God's truth in favor of their own sinful desires have no apologetic (or defense) for what they have done (Romans 2:1).

Reputable Christian Organizations

Athletes in Action www.aia.com

Campus Crusade for Christ www.ccci.org

Campus Outreach www.campusoutreach.org

Fellowship of Christian Athletes www.fca.org

International Students, Inc. www.isionline.org

Intervarsity Christian Fellowship www.intervarsity.org

Navigators www.navigators.org

Reformed University Fellowship www.ruf.org

Worldwide Discipleship Association www.disciplebuilding.org

Apologetics Web Sites

These are the best Web sites I know, but this list is by no means exhaustive. And, inclusion in this appendix doesn't mean that I agree with or endorse everything that you might find within these pages or on one of their links.

General Apologetics

www.4truth.net
www.allaboutgod.com
www.ankerberg.com
www.answering-islam.org
www.apologetics.com
www.apologeticsindex.org
www.beyondbelief.com
www.carm.org
www.christiananswers.net
www.christian-thinktank.com
www.designinference.com
www.equip.org
www.impactapologetics.com
www.josh.org
www.leestrobel.com

www.normangeisler.com
www.paulcopan.com
www.peterkreeft.com
www.rzim.org
www.str.org
www.tektonics.org
www.watchman.org

Ancient sources referencing Christianity

www.earlychristianwritings.com
www.ntcanon.org
www.scriptures.com

Atheism

www.answeringinfidels.com
www.ex-atheist.com

Biblical inerrancy

www.inerrancy.com

College student, teen outreach

www.boundless.org (excellent collection of articles, sponsored by
Focus on the Family)
www.trueU.org (awesome place to discover truth)

Creation and Evolution

www.answersingenesis.org

www.creationscience.com

www.icr.org

www.answersingenesis.org/Home/Area/bios/default.asp (Ever
     wondered if any scientists believe the book of Genesis?)

Cults

www.canauserworld.com (Web site of apologist
     Marcia Montenegro, a former wiccan)

www.christiananswers.net

www.ronrhodes.org

www.watchman.org

Resurrection of Christ

www.garyhabermas.com

www.risenjesus.com

A Suggested Reading List

Christians should read a lot. Drawing water from many wells will keep you from getting intellectually stagnant. Thomas Aquinas said, "Beware of the man of one book."[1] Of course, the Christian's number one read is the Bible. The claims of all other books must be measured against the content of God's written word. Or, as they say down South, "Learn how to eat the chicken and spit out the bones."

Old Guys but Good Guys

Confessions by Saint Augustine (Hendrickson Publishers, 2005). This book is often considered the "first spiritual autobiography" in Western literature.

Saint Thomas Aquinas by G. K. Chesterton (Doubleday, 2001). An inspiring account of the life of Aquinas, who taught that reason can be trusted.

Apologetics / Biblical Worldview

Baker Encyclopedia of Christian Apologetics by Norman L. Geisler, (Baker, 1999).

Fatal Flaws: What the Evolutionists Don't Want You to Know by Hank Hanegraaff (Nelson, 2003).

Handbook of Christian Apologetics by Peter Kreeft and Ron K. Tacelli (Intervarsity Press, 1994). Also recommended, condensed version of this excellent book, titled *Pocket Handbook of Christian Apologetics* (2003).

Stand: Core Truths You Must Know for an Unshakable Faith by Alex McFarland (Focus on the Family/Tyndale, 2005).

The Bible Answer Book for Students by Hank Hanegraaff (Nashville: Nelson, 2007).

The Case for a Creator by Lee Strobel (Zondervan, 2005).

The Case for Faith—Student Edition by Lee Strobel with Jean Vogel (Zondervan, 2002).

The Case for the Real Jesus by Lee Strobel (Zondervan, 2007).

The Consequences of Ideas by R. C. Sproul (Crossway, 2000).

The Historical Jesus: Ancient Evidence for the Life of Christ by Gary R. Habermas (College Press, 1996).

The New Evidence That Demands a Verdict by Josh McDowell (Nelson, 1999).

The Pilgrim's Regress by C. S. Lewis (Eerdmans, 1992).

The Ten Most Common Objections to Christianity by Alex McFarland (Regal, 2007).

The Universe Next Door by James W. Sire (InterVarsity, 2004).

The Victory of Reason: How Christianity Led to Freedom, Capitalism, and Western Success by Rodney Stark (Random House, 2006).

True for You, but Not for Me by Paul Copan (Bethany, 1998).

Christian Living

Becoming a Contagious Christian by Bill Hybels and Mark Mittelberg (Zondervan, 1996).

Destination Unknown: A Guide to Discovering God's Will by Gordon S. Jackson (NavPress, 2004).

Finding God at Harvard: Spiritual Journeys of Thinking Christians edited by Kelly Monroe Kullberg (InterVarsity, 2007).

Morning and Evening Devotions: Based on the New International Version by Charles H. Spurgeon (Hendrickson Publishers, 1995).

Smart Sex: Finding Life-Long Love in a Hook-up World by Jennifer Roback Morse (Spence Publishing, 2005).

The Fabric of This World: Inquiries into Calling, Career Choice, and the Design of Human Work by Lee Hardy (Eerdmans, 1990).

University of Destruction: Your Game Plan for Spiritual Victory on Campus by David Wheaten (Bethany, 2005).

Where Was God? by Erwin O. Lutzer (Tyndale, 2006).

Wired by God by Joe White with Larry Weeden (Focus on the Family\Tyndale, 2004).

Great Reads That Can't Be Categorized

5 Minute Church Historian by Rick Cornish (NavPress, 2005).

Leaving Home by Garrison Keillor (Penguin Books, 1997).

The Best Loved Poems of the American People edited by Hazel Felleman (Doubleday, 1936). This classic collection is still a best-seller.

Notes

Introduction

1. Frank Loesser, *Guys and Dolls* (New York: Music Theatre International, 1978), p. 111.

Chapter 1: Do You Have What It Takes?

1. Barna Research Group, "Life Goals of America's Teens," a study commissioned by Josh McDowell Ministry (Ventura, Calif.: The Barna Research Group, 2001), p. 6.
2. Josh McDowell, *The Last Christian Generation* (Holiday, Fla.: Green Key Books, 2006), p. 13.
3. George Barna, *Think Like Jesus* (Minneapolis, Minn.: Baker Books, 2003), p. 26.
4. The Barna Group, "Most Twentysomethings Put Christianity on the Shelf Following Spiritually Active Teen Years," September 11, 2006, http://www.barna.org/FlexPage.aspx?Page=BarnaUpdate&BarnaUpdateID=245.
5. Associated Press, "Report Flags Acute Homesickness," *Charlotte (NC) Observer,* January 2, 2007.
6. BrainyQuote.com, "William Butler Yeats Quotes," http://www.brainyquote.com/quotes/quotes/w/williambut101244.html.

Chapter 2: You Are Not Your Own

1. John Newton, "Amazing Grace" (1779).
2. Martin Luther, quoted in Randy Alcorn, "The Grace and Truth Paradox," Eternal Perspectives Ministries, http://www.epm.org/articles/Grace&Truth.htm.
3. James Sire, *The Universe Next Door* (Downers Grove, Ill.: Inter-Varsity, 1988), pp. 15-16.
4. *World Book Encyclopedia,* 1975 ed., s.v. "Magellan, Ferdinand (1480?-1521)."

Chapter 3: Emotional Stability

1. Mindy Fetterman, "Costly College Prerequisite: Decorate Dorm," *USA Today,* August 4, 2006.
2. The Quotations Page, "Quotations by Author," Woody Allen, http://www.quotationspage.com/quotes/Woody_Allen.
3. ThinkExist.com, "Paul Tillich quotes," http://thinkexist.com/quotation/language-has_created_the_word-loneliness-to/217971.html.

Chapter 4: Physical Disciplines

1. EW.com (*Entertainment Weekly*), "The 50 Best High School Movies," http://www.ew.com/ew/gallery/0,,1532588_3,00.html.
2. Wikipedia, "The Karate Kid," http://en.wikipedia.org/wiki/The_Karate_KidKarate Kid (accessed April 21, 2007).
3. Albert E. Grays, quoted in Shawn Covey, *7 Habits of Highly Effective Teens* (New York: Simon & Schuster, 1998), p. 125.
4. Theodore Roosevelt, quoted in Dave Ramsey, *More Than Enough* (New York: Penguin Books, 2002), p. 186.

Part Two: An Unshakable Faith

1. Josh McDowell, *Answers to Tough Questions* (San Bernardino, Calif.: Here's Life Publishers, 1980), pp. 9-10.
2. Ibid.

Chapter 5: Academic Readiness

1. C. S. Lewis, *Mere Christianity* (New York: Macmillan, 1960), p. 75.
2. John Godfrey Saxe, "Blind Men and the Elephant," http://www.wordinfo.info/words/index/info/view_unit/1/?letter=B&spage=3.
3. J. Budziszewski, *How to Stay Christian in College* (Colorado Springs, Colo.: NavPress, 2004), p. 49.
4. Norman Geisler and Frank Turek, *I Don't Have Enough Faith to Be an Atheist* (Wheaton, Ill.: Crossway, 2004), p. 27.
5. Paul Johnson, *Modern Times* (New York: Harper & Row, 1983), p. 11.
6. Chris Bull, "Theoretical Battles—Gay/Lesbian Studies Under Attack—Gay Activism in U.S. Colleges," *The Advocate,* September 29, 1998.
7. Ihab Hassan, "From Postmodernism to Postmodernity: the Local/Global Context," http://www.ihabhassan.com.
8. BrainyQuote.com, "Mark Twain Quotes," http://www.brainyquote.com/quotes/authors/m/mark_twain.html.
9. The Quotations Page, "René Descartes Quotes," http://www.quotationspage.com/quotes/Rene_Descartes.
10. Mortimer Adler, "The Technique of Philosophy," quoted in Robert B. Heywood, ed., *The Works of the Mind* (Chicago: University of Chicago Press, 1947), p. 216.

Chapter 6: Logic, Philosphy, and God

1. Carl Sagan, *Cosmos* (New York: Random House, 1980), p. 4.
2. Ibid.
3. Script-o-rama.com, "I, Robot Script—Dialogue Transcript," http://www.script-o-rama.com/movie_scripts/i/i-robot-script-tran script.html
4. The Internet Movie Script Database (IMSDb), "Contact Script," http://www.imsdb.com/scripts/Contact.html.
5. ThinkExist.com, "George Washington Carver quotes," http://thinkexist.com/quotation/reading_about_nature_is_fine-but_if_a_person/207960.html.
6. Wisdomquotes.com, "Truth Quotes," http://www.wisdom quotes.com/cat_truth.html.
7. C. S. Lewis, *The Abolition of Man* (New York: MacMillan, 1947), pp. 195-221.
8. Friedrich Nietzsche, *Thus Spake Zarathustra* (New York: Prometheus Books, 1993), p. 35.
9. Friedrich Nietzsche, *The Gay Science,* trans. Walter Kaufman (New York: Random House, 1974), p. 341.

Chapter 7: Attacks on Biblical Morality

1. John Keats, "Ode on a Grecian Urn," Bartleby.com, http://www.bartleby.com/126/41.html.
2. James Davison Hunter, *Culture Wars: The Struggle to Define America* (New York: Basic Books, 1991), pp. 215-216.
3. Ibid.

4. Ken Winters, "Gambling and College Students," Minnesota Institute of Public Health, http://www.miph.org/gambling/gmb_collegestud.html (accessed April 14, 2007). See also http://www.gamblinghelp.org.

5. Ncaa.org, "Sports Wagering: 2003 NCAA National Study on Collegiate Sports Wagering and Associated Behaviors," http://www.ncaa.org/library/research/sports_wagering/2003/2003_sports_wagering_study.pdf.

6. zaadz, "Quotes by Jonathan Edwards," http://quotes.zaadz.com/Jonathan_Edwards.

7. QuoteDB, "Authors: G. K. Chesterton," http://www.quotedb.com/quotes/493.

Chapter 8: Disciplines for Your Mind

1. ThinkExist.com, "Frank Herbert quotes," http://thinkexist.com/quotation/seek_freedom_and_become_captive_of_your_desires/205957.html.

2. *The President's Report of the Salk Institute for Biological Studies,* "Celebrating Two Giants of Molecular Biology," p. 1, http://www.salk.edu/news/publications/InsideSalk03_03.pdf (accessed April 21, 2007).

3. The Phrase Finder, "Genius is one percent inspiration and 99 percent perspiration," http://www.phrases.org.uk/meanings/146600.html.

4. Susan Conroy, *Mother Teresa's Lessons of Love and Secrets of Sanctity,* (Huntington, Ind.: Our Sunday Visitor, 2003), p. 10.

5. Bible.org, Sermon Illustrations, "Topic: Education," http://www.bible.org/illus.php?topic_id=457.

Chapter 9: Ethics

1. Alexander Graham Bell, quoted in Dave Ramsey, *More than Enough* (New York: Penguin, 2002), p. 55.
2. Wisdom Quotes, "Ethics Quotes," http://www.wisdom quotes.com/cat_ethics.html.
3. Amy Giffith, "Business Ethics Curriculum Builds Steam Among Colleges," *The City (Nashville) Paper,* November 6, 2006.

Chapter 10: Sexual Purity

1. Lauren Winner, *Real Sex: The Naked Truth About Chastity* (Grand Rapids, Mich.: Brazos Press, 2006), p. 16.
2. Ibid., pp. 37-38.
3. Ibid., p. 38.
4. J. Budziszewski, *How to Stay Christian in College* (Colorado Springs, Colo.: NavPress, 2004), p. 131.
5. Ted Bundy, interview by Dr. James Dobson, "Pornography Kills," *Focus on the Family Daily Broadcast,* February 2-3, 1989.
6. BrainyQuote.com, "Saint Augustine Quotes," http://www.brainyquote.com/quotes/quotes/s/saintaugus148557.html.

Chapter 11: Spiritual Adventures

1. Josh McDowell, *The Last Christian Generation* (Holiday, Fla.: Green Key Books, 2006), p. 13.
2. Erwin Lutzer, *The Backdoor to Success* (Chicago: Moody, 1987), p. 136.
3. Hadewijch, quoted in Larry Sibley, ed., *Classic Quotes on Contemporary Issues* (Wheaton, Ill.: Harold Shaw, 1997), p. 25.

Chapter 12: Life After College

1. IMDb, "Chariots of Fire," http://www.imdb.com/title/tt0082158.
2. BrainyQuote.com, "Helen Keller Quotes," http://www.brainy quote.com/quotes/authors/h/helen_keller.html.
3. BrainyQuote.com, "Abraham Lincoln Quotes," http://www .brainyquote.com/quotes/quotes/a/abrahamlin163082.html.

Appendix I: *Stand Strong* Answers 20 Questions

1. William Dembski and James M. Kushiner, eds., *Signs of Intelligence* (Grand Rapids, Mich.: Brazos Press, 2001), p. 108.
2. Ibid.
3. Geoffrey Simmons, *What Darwin Didn't Know* (Eugene, Ore.: Harvest House, 2004), pp. 52-53.
4. Robert Jastrow, *God and the Astronomers* (New York: Norton, 1992), p. 118.
5. Fred Hoyle, *The Intelligent Universe* (New York: Holt, Rinehart and Winston, 1983), p. 12.
6. N. Takahata, "A Genetic Perspective on the Origin and History of Humans," *Annual Review of Ecology and Systematics,* Annual Review, 26 (1995): pp. 343-372.
7. Whitey Hagadorn, quoted in Thomas Hayden, "A Theory Evolves," *U.S. News and World Report,* July 29, 2002, p. 45.

Appendix IV: Suggested Reading List

1. ThinkExist.com, "Saint Thomas Aquinas quotes," http://think exist.com/quotation/beware_the_man_of_one_book/12058.html.

FOCUS ^{ON}_{THE} FAMILY®

Welcome to the family!

Whether you purchased this book, borrowed it, or received it as a gift, we're glad you're reading it. It's just one of the many helpful, encouraging, and biblically based resources produced by Focus on the Family for people in all stages of life.

Focus began in 1977 with the vision of one man, Dr. James Dobson, a licensed psychologist and author of numerous best-selling books on marriage, parenting, and family. Alarmed by the societal, political, and economic pressures that were threatening the existence of the American family, Dr. Dobson founded Focus on the Family with one employee and a once-a-week radio broadcast aired on 36 stations.

Now an international organization reaching millions of people daily, Focus on the Family is dedicated to preserving values and strengthening and encouraging families through the life-changing message of Jesus Christ.

Focus on the Family Magazines

These faith-building, character-developing publications address the interests, issues, concerns, and challenges faced by every member of your family from preschool through the senior years.

| Focus on the Family **Citizen®** U.S. news issues | Focus on the Family **Clubhouse Jr.™** Ages 4 to 8 | Focus on the Family **Clubhouse™** Ages 8 to 12 | **Breakaway®** Teen guys | **Brio®** Teen girls 12 to 16 | **Brio & Beyond®** Teen girls 16 to 19 | **Plugged In®** Reviews movies, music, TV |

FOR MORE INFORMATION

 Online:
Log on to www.family.org
In Canada, log on to www.focusonthefamily.ca

 Phone:
Call toll free: (800) A-FAMILY (232-6459)
In Canada, call toll free: (800) 661-9800

BP06XFM

More Great Resources
from Focus on the Family®

Stand:
Core Truths You Must Know for
an Unshakable Faith
By Alex McFarland

Ready to know why our core beliefs are important to everyday life? Alex's first book *Stand* will get you off the roller coaster of doubt and on to solid ground. By understanding the purpose of Jesus Christ's life, death and resurrection, you can be ready to stand as a light in our dark world.

You're Next:
Outrageous Stories from My Life that
Could Change Yours
By Greg Stier

Like many teens, Greg grappled with big questions about God ... only how he arrived at answers was anything but normal. Truth made Greg a crazy man for God—and *You're Next*! These outrageous true stories will give you a taste of God's extreme love, which just might spread to your friends, family, and even strangers.

Pure Excitement:
A Godly Look at Sex, Love and Dating
By Joe White

Imagine you're in love ... head-over-heels and everything. Be equipped to make smart choices now to experience God's best for your life. Even if you've made mistakes, Joe's message is about hope. Learn the principles God sets for sex and intimacy to be the best—and to last a lifetime.

FOR MORE INFORMATION

 Online:
Log on to www.family.org
In Canada, log on to www.focusonthefamily.ca.

 Phone:
Call toll free: (800) A-FAMILY
In Canada, call toll free: (800) 661-9800.

BP06XP1

TAKE A STAND

with Alex McFarland

Free inspirational videos
from Alex McFarland

Watch Alex *free* online!

inspiration.net
Be Inspired

www.alexmcfarland.com

We're warned in Ephesians 4:14 to grow in our faith so that "we will no longer be infants, tossed back and forth by the waves, and blown here and there by every wind of teaching." Alex McFarland is gifted by God with the knowledge, urgency, and clarity needed to help prospective college students prepare for those inevitable waves.

—Mark Mittelberg, International Speaker and Coauthor
of *Becoming a Contagious Christian*

In the pages of this mind-illuminating, heart-piercing, and soul-enlarging book, Alex's infectious passion will give you the holistic resources to stand strong in college. And in your standing strong you will help others stand strong as well.

—Derwin L. Gray, Pastor, Evangelist, Author,
and "Evangelism Linebacker"

If there was ever a time to inoculate students against the anti-Christian viruses that circulate in the rarified air of college campus classrooms, that time is now. McFarland's *Stand Strong* is an effective antidote to a pandemic claiming the spiritual lives of tens of thousands of Christian kids who are leaving the biblical worldview and landing in a wasteland of pseudospirituality.

—Hank Hanegraaff, host of the *Bible Answer Man*
broadcast and author of *The Apocalypse Code*

Stand Strong is not just about surviving the post high school years. It's about having a solid faith that can withstand the intellectual and emotional challenges the world throws at you. I wish every young person would read this and take it to heart.

—Sean McDowell, Author of *ETHIX: Being Bold in a Whatever World*

While some are discussing why so many teens are falling by the wayside, Alex McFarland takes action. As students face the realities of temptation, deception, and distraction on the university campus, Alex offers practical guidance for staying grounded, growing deeper, and living with purpose and confidence during the college years. *Stand Strong in college* is a gift to a generation at risk.

—Ron Forseth, Vice President, Outreach, Inc. and General Manager, SermonCentral.com

Tyndale House Publishers, Inc.
Carol Stream, Illinois